ROUTLEDGE LIBRARY EDITIONS: LIBRARY AND INFORMATION SCIENCE

Volume 10

BIOCHEMISTRY COLLECTIONS

BIOCHEMISTRY COLLECTIONS
A Cross-Disciplinary Survey of the Literature

Edited by
BERNARD S. SCHLESSINGER

LONDON AND NEW YORK

First published in 1982 by The Haworth Press, Inc.

This edition first published in 2020
by Routledge
2 Park Square, Milton Park, Abingdon, Oxon OX14 4RN

and by Routledge
52 Vanderbilt Avenue, New York, NY 10017

Routledge is an imprint of the Taylor & Francis Group, an informa business

© 1982 The Haworth Press, Inc.

All rights reserved. No part of this book may be reprinted or reproduced or utilised in any form or by any electronic, mechanical, or other means, now known or hereafter invented, including photocopying and recording, or in any information storage or retrieval system, without permission in writing from the publishers.

Trademark notice: Product or corporate names may be trademarks or registered trademarks, and are used only for identification and explanation without intent to infringe.

British Library Cataloguing in Publication Data
A catalogue record for this book is available from the British Library

ISBN: 978-0-367-34616-4 (Set)
ISBN: 978-0-429-34352-0 (Set) (ebk)
ISBN: 978-0-367-43408-3 (Volume 10) (hbk)
ISBN: 978-0-367-43410-6 (Volume 10) (pbk)
ISBN: 978-1-00-300299-4 (Volume 10) (ebk)

Publisher's Note
The publisher has gone to great lengths to ensure the quality of this reprint but points out that some imperfections in the original copies may be apparent.

Disclaimer
The publisher has made every effort to trace copyright holders and would welcome correspondence from those they have been unable to trace.

Biochemistry Collections

A CROSS-DISCIPLINARY SURVEY OF THE LITERATURE

Bernard S. Schlessinger, Guest Editor

Special Collections
Volume 1, Number 2

The Haworth Press
New York

Special Collections, Volume 1, Number 2, Winter 1981.
Special Collections is published quarterly in the Fall, Winter, Spring, and Summer. Articles in this publication are abstracted in *Library & Information Science Abstracts.*
   EDITORIAL CORRESPONDENCE. Lee Ash, General Editor, 66 Humiston Drive, Bethany, CT 06525.
   BUSINESS OFFICE. All subscription and advertising inquiries should be directed to The Haworth Press, 28 East 22 Street, New York, NY 10010. Telephone (212) 228-2800.
   SUBSCRIPTIONS are on an academic year, per volume basis only. $85.00. Postage and handling: U.S. orders, add $1.75; Canadian orders, add $6.00 U.S. currency or $6.50 Canadian currency. Foreign rates: individuals, add $20.00; institutions, add $30.00; libraries, add $40.00 (includes postage and handling).
   CHANGE OF ADDRESS. Please notify the Subscription Department, The Haworth Press, 75 Griswold Street, Binghamton, NY 13904 of address changes. Please allow six weeks for processing; include old and new addresses, including ZIP codes.

Copyright © 1982 by The Haworth Press, Inc. All rights reserved. Copies of articles in this work may be noncommercially reproduced for the purpose of educational or scientific advancement. Otherwise, no part of this work may be reproduced or utilized in any form or by any means, electronic or mechanical, including photocopying, microfilm and recording, or by any information storage or retrieval system, without permission in writing from the publisher. Printed in the United States of America.

The Haworth Press, Inc., 28 East 22 Street, New York, NY 10010

Library of Congress Cataloging in Publication Data

Main entry under title

Biochemistry collections, a cross-disciplinary survey of
   the literature.

   (Special collections ; v. 1, no. 2)
   Includes bibliographies.
   1. Libraries—Special collections—Biological chemistry.   I. Schlessinger, Bernard S., 1930–
II. Series.
Z688.B54B56   026'.57419'2   81-13408
ISBN 0-917724-48-8   AACR2

Biochemistry Collections:
A Cross-Disciplinary Survey
of the Literature

Special Collections
Volume 1, Number 2

Foreword *Lee Ash, General Editor*	1
Biochemistry Subject Collections: An Introduction *Bernard S. Schlessinger, Guest Editor*	3
The History of Biochemistry: A Review of the Literature of the Field *Frederic L. Holmes*	7
Vignettes of Some Major Biochemistry Collections *Jill S. Smith*	17
Book Publishing in Biochemistry: Volume and Costs *Janice Sieburth*	27
Collection Development: Monographs for Biochemistry *Ann Knight Randall*	41
Collection Development: Journals for Biochemists *Tony Stankus*	51
Bibliographic Control: Indexing and Abstracting Services in Biochemistry—A Chronological and Historical Approach *Judith A. Douville*	75
Retrieval of Biochemical Information by Chemical Structure *Phillip Raoul Douville*	87
A Partial List of Some Biochemistry and Organic Chemistry Library Collections *Compiled by Lee Ash*	101

Notice: National Library of Medicine—Publication Grant
   Program for Biomedical Works   107

Books of Interest to Special Collections of All Kinds   109
               Compiled by Lee Ash

FOREWORD

This second issue of *Special Collections*, "Biochemistry Collections: A Cross-Disciplinary Survey of the Literature," offers a different approach to the subject than will be found in subsequent issues. Dean Schlessinger, the Guest Editor, and I determined early in planning for the Biochemistry issue that the subject is so new, relatively, that it has not yet developed a cohesive history, which Professor Holmes' excellent paper will easily indicate to any reader. The historic character will be of interest to special collections librarians, and others concerned with biochemistry and its related fields, has been developed with reference to the production, control, and use of the literature, as our specialist contributors have described it.

Further, because of the great diversity of the literature of the many special sciences that contribute to the subject biochemistry, and the variety of approaches necessary to consideration of it, we thought it better not to review publications of the past few years (other than in some remarks by Professor Holmes), as we have planned for other issues. There is, however, the usual review essay concerning books and other publications pertinent to special collections of all kinds.

Lee Ash
General Editor

66 Humiston Drive
Bethany, CT 06525

Correspondence and review copies of publications should be sent to this address.

BIOCHEMISTRY SUBJECT COLLECTIONS: AN INTRODUCTION

Bernard S. Schlessinger, Guest Editor

Biochemistry, the study of chemical processes in living things, has developed dramatically, within not much more than the past forty years, as the introduction of sophisticated analytical and computational tools has allowed the research emphasis to move from description and separation of chemical components of the cell to the study of changes occurring within the cell (Navia, 1975). At the same time, the importance of the discipline has increased enormously, with discoveries impacting on medicine and the secrets of the origin of life (Stryer, 1975).

The growth in interest in the discipline of biochemistry has been paralleled by a surge of research and of research literature in the field. For the serious literature researcher in biochemistry, this has forced a broadening of the awareness of peripheral fields, as well as a necessity to survey an increasingly larger number of citations.

One can appreciate the necessity for this broadening of the awareness of peripheral fields by looking at the chapter headings in one of the premier introductory texts in the field (Lehninger, 1975):

Biomolecules and Cells	Amino Acid Building Blocks of Protein
Water	
Proteins and Their Biological Functions	Proteins: Covalent Backbone and Amino Acid Sequence
Proteins: 3-Dimensional Conformation	Oxidation of Fatty Acids
Proteins: Purification and Characterization	Oxidative Degradation of Amino Acids

---

Bernard S. Schlessinger is Dean, Graduate Library School, University of Rhode Island, Kingston, RI 02881.

Enzymes: Kinetics and Inhibition

Enzymes: Mechanism, Structure and Regulation

Sugars, Storage Polysaccharides, and Cell Walls

Lipids, Lipoproteins and Membranes

Nucleotides and the Covalent Structure of Nucleic Acids

Vitamins and Co-enzymes

Metabolic and Energy-Transfer Pathways

Bioenergetic Principles Principles and the ATP Cycle

Glycolysis

The Tricarboxylic Acid Cycle and the Phosphogluconate Pathway

Oxidation-Reduction Enzymes and Electron Transport

Photosynthetic Electron Transport and Phosphorylation

Biosynthesis of Nucleotides

Biochemistry of Muscle and Motile Systems

Organ Interrelationships in the Metabolism of Mammals

DNA and the Structure of the Genetic Material

Replication and Transcription of DNA

Translation: The Biosynthesis of Proteins

The Genetic Code

Regulation of Gene Expression

Molecular Basis of Morphogenesis

Origin of Life

Oxidative Phosphorylation, Mitochondrial Structure, and the Compartmentation of Respiratory Metabolism

The same perception can be obtained by using the Sieburth (1980) definition of biochemistry to include "chemical work on living organisms; the study of substances such as proteins, nucleic acids, minerals and enzymes; the metabolism of these compounds; nitrogen fixation and photosynthesis and the chemical basis of disease... [and some studies dealing with] microbiology, immunology, pathology, endocrinology... [plus see also interest items from] acid-base equilibrium, biochemical genetics, chomatographic analysis, cytochemistry, metabolism, microbial metabolities, molecular biology, photosynthesis, physiological chemistry and radioisotopes..."

As for the volume of material to be covered, one need only look at representative figures, such as those for monographs [201 published by 25 major publishers in 1975 to 309 published in 1978 as reported by Sieburth (1980)] or for serials [three journals publishing more than 1,000 papers and a total production of 20–25,000 papers in 1979 as reported by Garfield (1979)].

Collection development and information retrieval in a field as important and as vigorous as biochemistry are challenging for any librarian entrusted with providing access to the information in the discipline. The several papers which follow this introduction attempt to provide aids for such librarians/selectors.

Lee Ash suggests that Professor Holmes' paper, the first, is of such unusual quality and so successfully reviews the historical literature that it deserves elevation to the character of a "classic" of medicine and science. It is a most remarkable contribution and deserves the close attention of our readers.

In the second paper, Jill Smith includes vignettes of ten major biochemistry collections representing a geographic and type-of-library range. For most, some elements of both history and size are included.

Janice Sieburth analyzes volume and cost of books published in biochemistry between 1975 and 1979, using various sources for data. In addition to statistics, her paper includes a list of the 65 publishers who produced biochemical books in that period, as well as the 25 largest publishers for the period.

Ann Randall, in treating collection development for monographs, provides some basic guidelines for selection, presents an analysis that relates the ratios of citations to budget allocations for monographs and serials, and reviews automated advances that impact on collection development. This is followed by descriptions of selection sources (general announcement services, book review media, and other aids).

Collection development for journals is discussed by Tony Stankus, who first spends time with historical developments and classifications of serials. The two schools of scientific journal collection development are also treated. Through analysis of where American biochemists publish, authorship of articles in selected journals, publication practices of authors in for-profit firms and in small liberal arts colleges, and journals most frequently cited in texts, a list of journals important for collection development is generated.

Judith Douville presents a descriptive overview of the indexing and abstract services important to biochemistry, present and past. Both traditional and on-line bibliographic services are included.

Retrieval by the use of chemical structure is discussed by Phillip Douville. Traditional manual methods and their computerized relatives are included, as are two newer methods of indexing and retrieval (the Wiswesser Notation, to which an introduction is given, and Derwent's fragmentation codes).

Finally, the General Editor, Lee Ash, presents a potpourri of reviews, listing, news, and notices of publications received, of interest to Special Collections librarians in all kinds of libraries.

REFERENCES

Garfield, Eugene. "Trends in Biochemical Literature." *Trends in Biochemical Sciences, 1979, 4,* 290–3.
Lehninger, Albert. *Biochemistry.* New York: Worth, 1978.
Navia, Juan. "Biochemistry." In *Americana.* New York: Americana Corporation, 1975.
Sieburth, Janice. "Book Publishing in Biochemistry." In *Biochemistry Subject Collections.* New York: Haworth, 1980.
Stryer, Lubert. *Biochemistry.* San Francisco: Freeman and Co., 1975.

THE HISTORY OF BIOCHEMISTRY: A REVIEW OF THE LITERATURE OF THE FIELD

Frederic L. Holmes

As a formal scientific discipline, biochemistry has emerged during the twentieth century. Some of the phenomena included within its modern domain have, however, been thought about and investigated for much longer. Within the Western scientific tradition the classic Greek writers, including the authors of the Hippocratic treatises, Aristotle, and Galen, gave much attention to digestion and nutrition, defined as the transformation of foodstuffs into the substance of the body. When chemistry emerged as a distinct field of operations and doctrines during the seventeenth century, theoretical applications were quickly made to explain these same physiological processes. The decisive demarcation of the beginning of the modern field of experimental investigation took place at the end of the eighteenth century when Antoine Lavoisier applied his quantitative methods of chemical analysis and his new knowledge of the composition of water, air, and carbon dioxide to make the first determinations of the elementary compositions of substances derived from plants and animals, and when he utilized the same methods, together with direct calorimetric experiments on animals, to demonstrate that respiration is a form of slow combustion. On the first of these foundations the field of organic chemistry grew to a flourishing enterprise by the 1830s. Gradually, however, organic chemists departed from their original preoccupation with biologically significant substances, and another fledgling field, known as physiological chemistry, appeared to fill this gap. For the rest of the century, however, physiological chemistry remained, with a few notable exceptions, an adjunct to physiology.

At the beginning of the twentieth century several striking advances—the clarification of the structure of proteins, carbohydrates, and other biologically significant compounds through the work of Emil Fischer;

Frederic L. Holmes is Professor of the History of Medicine, Yale University School of Medicine, New Haven, CT 06510.

the recognition that very complex molecules, such as the proteins, are broken down into simpler *Bausteine* which undergo the central processes of metabolism; new successes in investigating the intermediary steps of metabolism; and the discovery by Eduard Buchner of cell-free fermentation, which gave a strong boost to the enzyme theory of life—together added great impetus to the development of physiological chemistry. Frequently, though not everywhere, the field was renamed biochemistry. During the first third of this century biochemistry acquired a firm institutional structure and became one of the dominant fields of scientific activity.

In comparison with the vast scope of the science of biochemistry itself, the literature on its history is sparse. Few individual biochemists or special areas of investigation have been studied in depth. Recently, however, interest in the history of biochemistry has been rising, and important initial forays have been made.

Among the general treatments of the subject, Henry Leicester's *Development of Biochemical Concepts from Ancient to Modern Times*[51] is the most accessible to the ordinary reader. This short book provides useful, though brief, descriptions of the most prominent landmarks in the long development of the subject from the earliest known speculations to the research of the 1930s. More authoritative and more detailed, though still highly selective, is Joseph Fruton's *Molecules and Life,*[23] which traces the thought and investigations of the central problems in biochemistry—fermentation, the nature of enzymes, the structure of proteins and of the nucleic acids, and the pathways of metabolism—from 1800 until the mid-twentieth century. Fruton's deep knowledge of his subject and the reliability of his historical work make this volume the best single guide to the history of the field, defined in terms of its ongoing areas of research. Marcel Florkin's multi-volume *History of Biochemistry*[19,20,21] is more encyclopedic, less selective, and less penetrating, but it is a rich source of information and contains an excellent collection of photographs of prominent biochemists. The earliest full-length history of biochemistry, Fritz Lieben's *Geschichte der Physiologischen Chemie* (1935),[52] described in great detail the chemical investigations of the nineteenth and early twentieth century upon which the field had by then been established. *The Chemistry of Life,* edited by Joseph Needham,[61] presents capsule histories of eight different problem areas within or related to biochemistry. These were originally lectures given as parts of a course in the history of science at the University of Cambridge, by biochemists whose own fields of interest parallel the historical problems they describe. Sections on the history of biochemistry are also contained in Aaron Ihde's *The Development of Modern Chemistry*,[35] and much information on the earlier developments can be gleaned from the volumes of J.R. Partington's massive *History of Chemistry*.[63]

Three divergent general interpretations of the historical formation of biochemistry have recently appeared. In an article on "The emergence of biochemistry,"[24] Fruton has portrayed the modern field evolving gradually out of a group of problems clearly defined during the nineteenth century and investigated continuously since then. Robert Kohler has argued, on the other hand,[42] that biochemistry represented a sharp departure from the older physiological chemistry and that it coalesced around the enzyme theory of life during the first decade of the twentieth century. Mikulas Teich has viewed the "rise of modern biochemistry" as a process involving "three stages of development: (i) a gradual separation of the science of chemistry of life from the general body of chemistry into organic chemistry (c. 1800–1840); (ii) a linking of organic chemistry with physiology (c. 1840–1880); and (iii) the separation of modern biochemistry from physiology."[70]

Since 1970 there have been five symposia on topics within the history of biochemistry, the proceedings of which were subsequently published. Two were sponsored by the American Academy of Arts and Science, the first being on "The History of Biochemistry and Molecular Biology,"[1] the second on "The Historical Development of Bioenergetics."[2] A symposium in honor of Severo Ochoa was held in 1976,[49] and a "Retrospect on Proteins" was held in 1978 under the auspices of the New York Academy of Sciences.[68] In 1979 a symposium on "Aspects of the History of Biochemistry" was included for the first time in the annual meeting of the Federation of American Societies for Experimental Biology.[16] The papers presented in these meetings were mostly by biochemists reflecting on developments within problem areas in which they themselves had participated. The character of their contributions ranged from informal reminiscences to careful historical analyses. A small number of papers presented by historians is also included in these collections.

Richard Willstätter,[75] Erwin Chargaff,[6] and Fritz Lipmann[53] have written autobiographies. Every year since 1953 an autobiographical essay by an eminent biochemist has appeared in *Annual Review of Biochemistry*. Frederick Gowland Hopkins, the founder of the Cambridge School of biochemistry, was the subject of a book entitled *Hopkins and Biochemistry*.[60] This volume contains essays on his personality and influence by former students and colleagues, an autobiographical sketch, and some of the well-known lectures in which Hopkins lucidly formulated the principles and prospects of his field.

Very few full-length biographies of biochemists exist. D.L. Drabkin wrote one of the life of the German-born English physiological chemist Thudicum.[11] The distinguished biochemist Sir Hans Krebs has expanded his Royal Society Obituary of his mentor, Otto Warburg, into a biography.[50] This exemplary study includes an authoritative summary of the scientific achievements which made Warburg the dominant figure in the field between 1925 and 1940, and a sensitive portrait of the rather overpowering, idiosyncratic personality of Warburg.

Several biochemists have carried out historical studies of subjects oriented toward their own special scientific interest, but extending well beyond their personal involvements. David Keilin's *The History of Cell Respiration and Cytochrome*[39] not only relates the events leading up to his initial discovery of the cytochromes, but places his work into the broader background of investigations of the respiratory process into which these compounds fit. Hermann Kalckar made important contributions to the field of "biological phosphorylations," the processes central to the means by which organisms convert into usable form the energy they derive from foodstuffs. In 1969 Kalckar published a collection of the original scientific papers representing basic landmarks in the development of this subject, some of which he translated into English.[38] Dorothy Needham, an important participant in the field of muscle metabolism, published in 1971 a magisterial history of that subject,[59] summarizing in close detail the major scientific contributions of the nineteenth and twentieth centuries. Hubert Vickery utilized his own extended experience in protein analysis to elucidate nineteenth-century investigations of proteins, especially the discoveries of the amino acids which compose them.[72] John Edsall, another major contributor to the chemistry of proteins, has written several articles analysing the historical evolution of concepts and investigations of those complex substances during the early twentieth century.[13,14,15,17]

Many histories of seventeenth-century science discuss aspects of the application of the new chemical concepts of that period to biological problems. A standard description of the chemical theories of digestion and nutrition is in Michael Foster's *Lectures on the History of Physiology*,[22] first published in 1901. A more recent interpretation of these and related chemical physiological theories is contained in Audrey Davis' *Circulation Physiology and Medical Chemistry in England, 1650–1680*.[8] Among the few recent studies of plant and animal chemistry during the eighteenth century is E.F. Beach's account of the discovery of gluten by Beccari;[4] F.R. Jevon's summary of the "biochemistry" of the very influential teacher of medicine in Leiden, Herman Boerhaave;[36] and F.L. Holmes' study of the gradual transformation in the methods and concepts used in the separation and identification of the constituent substances of plant and animal matter.[31] A significant new book by Reinhard Löw analyzes in detail the development of the special area of plant chemistry from the time of Lavoisier to that of Liebig in the 1830s.[54] June Goodfield[26] and Everett Mendelsohn[57] have given two rather different accounts of the evolution of the problem of respiration and animal heat during the late eighteenth and early nineteenth century. R.P. Aulie,[3] D.C. Goodman,[27] and F.L. Holmes[29,30,33] have written about various aspects of the application of chemical methods to physiological problems during the same period. Nikolas Mani's article on Friedrich Tiedemann and Leopold Gmelin[55] highlights the first intensive direct investigation of the physiological processes related to nutrition to be based on the new methods of chemical extraction and identification available in the early nineteenth century. A number of historians, including M.D. Grmek,[28] C. Debru,[9] G.F. Young[76] J. Schiller,[66] and F.L. Holmes,[32] have written about the physiological investigations of Claude Bernard related to chemical processes.

Robert Kohler has recently set forth a program for a history of biochemistry which would be oriented not around the research problems within the field, but toward the social context, especially the institutional settings, within which the science itself has developed. He discussed his general point of view in 1975 in an article entitled "The History of Biochemistry: A Survey,"[45] In other articles he has tried to show how nodal events such as Buchner's discovery of cell-free fermentation,[40,41] Harden's and Young's discovery of the role of phosphates in fermentation,[44] and Schoenheimer's use of isotopes to trace metabolic exchanges[46] can be understood within such a framework. The most successful demonstrations of his approach are his two latest studies, "Walter Fletcher, F.G. Hopkins, and the Dunn Institute of Biochemistry,"[47] and "Warren Weaver and the Rockefeller Foundation Program in Molecular Biology."[48]

Several descriptions of the development of biochemistry in particular places are available. Among the most interesting of these is the chapter "Physiologische Chemie" in Hans-Heinz Eulner's book on the history of medical specialities within German-speaking universities.[18] Eulner describes the various institutional arrangements, most of which subordinated the subject to physiology or medicine, that prevailed until the 1930s in Germany. Ironically, German biochemists attained leadership in the field during the very period when their professional position was quite insecure. Other studies of local biochemical developments are Russell Chittenden's book, *The Development of Physiological Chemistry in the United States* (1930),[7] and articles on the history of the subject in Germany,[67] in Berlin, in Liverpool,[58] in Cambridge,[77] and in Japan.[10]

Molecular biology, a scientific specialty which originated during the 1950s, overlaps so extensively with biochemistry that much controversy has arisen over whether it has been justified to designate it as a separate field. A number of recent books and articles deal with the sources and growth of molecular biology. Robert Olby's *The Path to the Double Helix*[62] describes in detail the various research strands—the development of the macromolecular concept, the recognition that nucleic acids rather than proteins may constitute the hereditary material; the demonstration of genetic transformations in bacteria, the migration of physicists and chemists into biological investigations—upon which James Watson and Francis Crick built to arrive at their famous discovery of the structure of DNA. In *A Century of DNA*,[64] Franklin Portugal and Jack Cohen add to the story Olby has told some aspects of the early history of the chemistry of the nucleic acids, but in other respects their account is less adequate. Horace Judson's remarkable book *The Eighth Day of Creation*[37] not only contributes a fresh perspective to the story of the discovery of the double helix, but traces the development of molecular biology further forward to the solution of the problem of the genetic code, the determination of the three-dimensional structure of protein, and other very recent advances. Prominently featured in this account are the personal interviews Judson carried out with numerous participants in these events. The book also succeeds extraordinarily well in making complex scientific ideas clear and concrete for the general reader, without distorting them. The best known book on the foundations of molecular biology is, of course James Watson's *The Double Helix*,[74] a highly subjective, revealing memoir about the personal activities of Crick, himself, and their associates while they were on the way toward their spectacular discovery. Those who have read this fascinating, provocative book should look also at Anne Sayre's *Rosalind Franklin and DNA* for an assessment of the contribution of Franklin to the discovery which differs sharply from that of Watson. Although Sayre's writing is colored by a passionate sense that Franklin was treated unfairly, she has drawn attention to ethical problems inherent in the events and their aftermath which cannot lightly be dismissed.[65]

Biochemistry has, from its origins, interacted closely with other fields such as immunology, endocrinology, bacteriology, pharmacology, and physiology. A description of the historical writings dealing with these areas is beyond the scope of the present article. Kohler's recent review of the state of the history of biochemistry includes a discussion of the literature in these areas.[45]

Joseph Fruton has provided a highly useful bibliography of biographical information about biochemists who have lived since 1800, as published in biographical dictionaries, eulogies, and other forms.[25] A valuable new research tool for scholars in the history of biochemistry and related sciences is the *Archival Sources for the History of Biochemistry and Molecular Biology*.[5] This volume contains information on personal archival collections of 595 scientists, of records, biochemical departments, funding agencies and other institutions, and indexes to both archival and bibliographical information on many individual scientists. This information is the outcome of a six-year survey project sponsored by the American Academy of Arts and Sciences and the American Philosophical Society. The volume includes instructions for obtaining further information gathered by the survey and stored by computer at the APS.

BIBLIOGRAPHY

1. The American Academy of Arts and Sciences. May 1970. *Proceedings of the Conference on the History of Biochemistry and Molecular Biology*. Brookline, Massachusetts.
2. The American Academy of Arts and Sciences. October 1973. *Proceedings of the Conference on the Historical Development of Bioenergetics*. Boston, Massachusetts.
3. Aulie, Richard P. "Boussingault and the Nitrogen Cycle." Reprint from *Proceedings of the American Philosophical Society* 114(1970):435–479.
4. Beach, Eliot F. "Beccari of Bologna: The Discoverer of Vegetable Protein." *Journal of the History of Medicine*, 16(1961):361–363.
5. Bearman, David and Edsall, John T., eds. *Archival Sources for the History of Biochemistry and Molecular Biology*. Ann Arbor, Michigan: University Microfilms International, 1980.
6. Chargaff, Erwin. *Heraclitean Fire: Sketches from a Life before Nature*. New York: Rockefeller University Press, 1978.
7. Chittenden, Russell H. *The Development of Physiological Chemistry in the United States*. New York: The Chemical Catalog Company, Inc., 1930.
8. Davis, Audrey B. *Circulation Physiology and Medical Chemistry in England 1650–1680*. Lawrence, Kansas: Coronado Press, 1973.
9. Debru, Claude. "Claude Bernard et l'idée d'une chimie biologique." *Rev. Hist. Sci.*, xxxii/2(1979):143–153.
10. Doke, T. "Establishment of Biochemistry in Japan." *Japanese Studies in the History of Science*, 8(1969):145–153.
11. Drabkin, D. L. *Thudicum: Chemist of the Brain*. Philadelphia: University of Penn. Press, 1958.

12. Dubos, René J. *The Professor, The Institute, and DNA.* New York: The Rockefeller University Press, 1976.
13. Edsall, John T. "Blood and Hemoglobin: The Evolution of Knowledge of Functional Adaptation in a Biochemical System." *Journal of the History of Biology,* 5(1972): 205–257.
14. Edsall, John T. *Some Early History of Cold-Insoluble Globulin.* Reprint from Annals of the New York Academy of Sciences, 312(1978):1–10. New York: The New York Academy of Sciences, 1978.
15. Edsall, John T. *The Development of the Physical Chemistry of Proteins, 1898–1940.* Annals New York Academy of Sciences, 325(1979):53–74.
16. Edsall, John T. "Introduction." In *Aspects of the history of Biochemistry:* 63rd Annual Meeting of the Federation of American Societies for Experimental Biology. Dallas, Texas: April 2, 1979.
17. Edsall, John T. "Hemoglobin and the Origins of the Concept of Allosterism." *Federation Proceedings* Vol. 39, 1980.
18. Eulner, Hans-Heinz. "Physiologische Chemie." *Die Entwicklung der medizinischen Spezialächer and den Universitäten des deutschen Sprachgebietes.* Stuttgart: Ferdinand Enke Verlag, 1970.
19. Florkin, Marcel. *A History of Biochemistry.* Part III. *History of the Identification of the Sources of Free Energy in Organisms.* Comprehensive Biochemistry, edited by Marcel Florkin and Elmer H. Stotz, vol. 31. Elsevier Scientific Publishing Company, 1975.
20. Florkin, Marcel. *A History of Biochemistry.* Part IV. *Early Studies on Biosynthesis.* Comprehensive Biochemistry, edited by Marcel Florkin and Elmer H. Stotz, vol. 32. Elsevier Scientific Publishing Company, 1977.
21. Florkin, Marcel. *A History of Biochemistry.* Part V. *The Unravelling of Biosynthetic Pathways.* Comprehensive Biochemistry, 2 vols. Amsterdam/Oxford/New York: Elsevier Scientific Publishing Company, 1979.
22. Foster, Michael. *Lectures on the History of Physiology during the Sixteenth, Seventeenth and Eighteenth Centuries.* Cambridge: Cambridge University Press, 1901.
23. Fruton, Joseph S. *"Molecules and Life": Historical Essays on the Interplay of Chemistry and Biology.* Wiley-Interscience, 1972.
24. Fruton, Joseph S. "The Emergence of Biochemistry." *Science,* 192(1976):327–334.
25. Fruton, Joseph S. *Selected Bibliography of Biographical Data for the History of Biochemistry since 1800.* 2d ed. Philadelphia: American Philosophical Society Library Publication No. 7, 1977.
26. Goodfield, G. June. *The Growth of Scientific Physiology: Physiological Method and the Mechanist-vitalist Controversy.* London: Hutchinson, 1960.
27. Goodman, D. C. "Chemistry and the Two Organic Kingdoms of Nature in the Nineteenth Century." *Medical History,* XVI(1972):113–130.
28. Grmek, M. D. "First Steps in Claude Bernard's Discovery of the Glycogenic Function of the Liver." *Journal of the History of Biology* 1(1968):141–154.
29. Holmes, Frederic L. "Elementary Analysis and the Origins of Physiological Chemistry." *ISIS,* 54(1963):50–81.
30. Holmes, Frederic L. "Introduction." *Animal Chemistry: The Sources of Science, No. 4,* by Justus Liebig. New York and London: Johnson Reprint Corporation, 1964.
31. Holmes, Frederic L. "Analysis by Fire and Solvent Extractions: The Metamorphosis of a Tradition." *ISIS,* 62(1970):129–148.
32. Holmes, Frederic Lawrence. *Claude Bernard and Animal Chemistry: The Emergence of a Scientist.* Cambridge, Massachusetts: Harvard University Press, 1974.
33. Holmes, Frederic L. "The Transformation of the Science of Nutrition." *Journal of the History of Biology* 8(1975):135–144.

34. Holmes, Frederic L. "Hans Krebs and the Discovery of the Ornithine Cycle." In *Aspects of the History of Biochemistry:* Federation Proc. 39(1980):216–225.
35. Ihde, Aaron J. *The Development of Modern Chemistry.* New York/Evanston/London: Harper & Row, 1964.
36. Jevons, F. R. "Boerhaave's Biochemistry." *Medical History* VI(1962):343–362.
37. Judson, Horace Freeland. *"The Eighth Day of Creation": The Makers of the Revolution in Biology.* New York: Simon and Schuster, 1979.
38. Kalckar, Herman M. *Biological Phosphyorylations: Development of Concepts.* Edited by William D. McElroy and Carl P. Swanson. New Jersey: Prentice-Hall, Inc., 1969.
39. Keilin, David. *The History of Cell Respiration and Cytochrome.* Prepared for Publication by Joan Keilin. Cambridge University Press, 1966.
40. Kohler, Robert. "The Background to Eduard Buchner's Discovery of Cell-Free Fermentation." *Journal of the History of Biology* 4(1971):35–61.
41. Kohler, Robert E. "The Reception of Eduard Buchner's Discovery of Cell-Free Fermentation." *Journal of the History of Biology,* 5(1972):327–353.
42. Kohler, Robert E. Jr. "The Enzyme Theory and the Origin of Biochemistry." *ISIS* 64(1973):181–196.
43. Kohler, Robert E. "The Background to Otto Warburg's Conception of the Atmungsferment." *Journal of the History of Biology* 6(1973):171–192.
44. Kohler, Robert E. "The background to Arthur Harden's discovery of Cozymase." *Bulletin of the History of Medicine* 48(1974):22–40.
45. Kohler, Robert E. "The History of Biochemistry: A Survey." *Journal of the History of Biology* 8(1976):275–318.
46. Kohler, Robert E. Jr. *Rudolf Schoenheimer, Isotopic Tracers, and Biochemistry in the 1930's.* Historical Studies in the Physical Sciences. Vol. 8, Russell McCormmach and Lewis Pyenson, Eds. Baltimore/London: The Johns Hopkins University Press, 1977.
47. Kohler, Robert E. "Walter Fletcher, F.G. Hopkins, and the Dunn Institute of Biochemistry: A Case Study in the Patronage of Science." *ISIS* 69(1978):331–355.
48. Kohler, Robert E. "Warren Weaver and the Rockefeller Foundation Program in Molecular Biology: A Case Study in the Management of Science." *The Sciences in the American Context: New Perspectives,* Nathan Reingold Ed., Smithsonian Institution Press, 1979:249–293.
49. Kornberg, A.; Horecker, B.L.; Cornudella, L.; and Oro, J., editors. *"Reflections on Biochemistry": In honour of Severo Ochoa.* Pergamon Press, 1976.
50. Krebs, Hans. *Otto Warburg. Zellphysiologer, Biochemiker, Mediziner, 1883–1970.* 1979 Reprint vol. 205. Stuttgart, Wissenschaftliche Verlagsgesellschaft, 1979.
51. Leicester, Henry M. *Development of Biochemical Concepts from Ancient to Modern Times.* Cambridge, Massachusetts: Harvard University Press, 1974.
52. Lieben, Dr. Fritz. *Geschichte Der Physiologischen Chemie.* Leipzig und Wien: Franz Deuticke, 1935.
53. Lipmann, Fritz. *Wanderings of a Biochemist.* Wiley-Interscience, 1971.
54. Löw, Reinhard. "Pflanzenchemie Zwischen Lavoisier und Liebig." *Münchener Hochschulschriften Reihe: Naturwissenschaften* Band 1. Straubing und München: Donau-Verlag, 1977.
55. Mani, Nikolaus. "Das Werk von Friedrich Tiedemann und Leopold Gmelin: 'Die Verdauung nach Versuchen' und sein Bedeutung für die Entwicklung der Ernährungslehre in der ersten Hälfte des 19. Jahrhunderts." *Gesnerus* 13(1956):200–207.
56. Mani, Nikolaus. *Die historischen Grundlagen der Leberforschung.* Basel/Stuttgart: Schwabe & Co., 1967.
57. Mendelsohn, Everett. *Heat and Life: The Development of the Theory of Animal Heat.* Cambridge, Massachusetts: Harvard University Press, 1964.
58. Morton, R.A. "Biochemistry at Liverpool 1902–1971." *Medical History* XVI (1972):321–353.

59. Needham, Dorothy M. *"Machina Carnis"*: *The Biochemistry of Muscular Contraction in its Historical Development*. Cambridge University Press, 1971.

60. Needham, Joseph; and Baldwin, Ernest; editors. *Hopkins & Biochemistry 1861–1947*. Cambridge: W. Heffer and Sons Limited, 1949.

61. Needham, Joseph, ed. *The Chemistry of Life:* Eight Lectures on the History of Biochemistry. Cambridge at the University Press, 1970.

62. Olby, Robert. *The Path to the Double Helix*. Seattle: University of Washington Press, 1974.

63. Partington, J.R. *A History of Chemistry*, I, II, III, and IV. London: MacMillan & Co., 1961–70.

64. Portugal, Franklin H., and Cohen, Jack S. *"A Century of DNA"*: *A History of the Discovery of the Structure and Function of the Genetic Substance*. Cambridge, Massachusetts: The MIT Press, 1977.

65. Sayre, Anne. *"Rosalind Franklin & DNA."* *A Vivid View of What It Is Like to Be a Gifted Woman in an Especially Male Profession*. New York: W.W. Norton & Company, Inc., 1975.

66. Schiller, Joseph. *Claude Bernard: et les Problèmes Scientifiques de son Temps*. Paris: Les Editions du Cèdre, 1967.

67. Simmer, Hans. "Aus den Anfängen der physiologischen Chemie in Deutschland." *Sudhoffs Archiv* 39(1955):216–236.

68. Srinivasan, P.R.; Fruton, Joseph S.; and Edsall, John T., editors. *The Origins of Modern Biochemistry: A Retrospect on Proteins*. Annals of the New York Academy of Sciences, Vol. 325. 1979.

69. Teich, Mikuláš. "From 'Enchyme' to 'Cyto-Skeleton': The Development of Ideas on the Chemical Organization of Living Matter." In *Changing Perspectives in the History of Science*, edited by Mikuláš Teich and Robert Young, pp. 439–471. London: Heinemann.

70. Teich, Mikuláš. "On the Historical Foundations of Modern Biochemistry." *Clio Medica* 1(1965):41–57. Great Britain: Pergamon Press Ltd.

71. Teich, Mikuláš. "The History of Modern Biochemistry. The Second Phase: C. 1920–1940/45." In *XIIe Congres International d'Histoire des Sciences*, pp. 199–203. Paris: Librairie Scientifique et Technique, 1968.

72. Vickery, Hubert B., and Schmidt, C.L.A. "The History of The Discovery of the Amino Acids." *Chemical Reviews* 9(1931):169–318.

73. Vickery, Hubert B. "The Origin of the Word Protein." *Yale Journal of Biology and Medicine* 22(1950):387–393.

74. Watson, James D. *"The Double Helix"*: A Personal Account of the Discovery of the Structure of DNA. New York: Atheneum, 1969.

75. Willstätter, Richard. *Aus meinem Leben*. A. Stall, ed. Weinheim: Verlag, Chemie, 1949.

76. Young, F.G. "Claude Bernard and the Theory of the Glycogenic Function of the Liver." *Annals of Science* 2(1937):47–83.

77. Young, F.G. "The Rise of Biochemistry in the Nineteenth Century, with Particular Reference to the University of Cambridge." *Cambridge and its Contribution to Medicine*. A.J. Rook, ed., pp. 155–172, Wellcome Institute of the History of Medicine, 1971.

VIGNETTES OF SOME MAJOR BIOCHEMISTRY COLLECTIONS

Jill S. Smith

The sketches included in this collection are of libraries selected by perusal of longer lists of major collections contained in two sources— *Subject Collections,* 5th edition, edited by Lee Ash (1978), and *Directory of Special Libraries and Information Centers,* edited by Margaret L. Young (1977). The libraries surveyed were chosen to represent only 2 geographic and type-of-library range and demonstrate a variety of character and origins.

To develop the data needed, the group of selected libraries was sent a letter and questionnaire which asked for specific information, including the names of the library and the librarian, the history of the collection, and the sizes of the monograph and periodical collection.

The vignettes which follow were prepared for those libraries which agreed to participate and are based on information which the participating libraries were willing to share. A more complete address list will be found in the Directory Chapter of this volume.

1. BECKMAN INSTRUMENTS
   A. Name of Library
      Research Library
      Beckman Instruments
      2500 Harbor Blvd.
      Fullerton, California 92634
   B. Name of Librarian
      Jean R. Miller
   C. History and Development of the Collection
      The library was officially begun in 1955, although the biochemistry collection has seen major growth primarily within the last ten years. This is due to the company's increasing emphasis on clinical and diagnostic instrumentation and biological and fine chemicals.

Jill Smith is Library Consultant, Princeton, NJ 08540.

D. Monograph Collection
      The total collection is approximately 375 volumes. Half of this total is retained by individuals in their respective offices.
   E. Periodical Collection
      The library subscribes to approximately 75 titles in the Biochemistry area. Additional subscriptions are placed for individuals within the company and are sent directly to them. There are 65 such subscriptions, about half of which duplicate the library's titles.
   F. Specially Noteable Features
      Journals in the field of Immunology and Clinical Chemistry are the main areas of interest.

2. COLD SPRING HARBOR LABORATORY
   A. Name of Library
      Cold Spring Harbor Laboratory, The Library
      P.O. Box 100
      Cold Spring Harbor, New York 11724
   B. Name of Librarian
      Susan Gensel, Head Librarian
      Audrey Bevington, Librarian
   C. History and Development of Collection
      The laboratory was founded by Brooklyn Institute of Arts and Sciences (BIAS) in 1890, as a summer Biology Study Program. In 1906, Carnegie Institute of Washington established the Station for Experimental Evolution (later called the Department of Genetics), running concurrently with BIAS until 1924. In 1924, the Long Island Biological Association took over the summer program from BIAS. In 1963 these areas either combined or dissolved to form Cold Spring Harbor Laboratory. The research emphasis has been on the biochemistry of genetics, molecular biology, cancer research, and virology.
   D. Monograph Collection
      The Main Library has 1900 biochemistry monographs, the Branch Virology Library 313, and the Banbury Conference Center Library-Biological Risk Assessment 262, for a total of 2,475 monographs.
   E. Periodical Collection
      The Main Library has 470 periodical titles in biochemistry, the Branch Virology Library has 33, and the Banbury Conference Center Library-Biological Risk Assessment has 48, for a total of 551 titles.

F. Specially Noteable Features
   The Library is postgraduate level in nature.

3. HARVARD UNIVERSITY
   A. Name of Library
      Biological Laboratories Library
      Harvard University
      16 Divinity Avenue
      Cambridge, Massachusetts 02138
   B. Name of Librarian
      Dorothy J. Solbrig
   C. History and Development of the Collection
      The Biological Laboratories Library is a departmental library which serves part of the Department of Biology and part of the Department of Biochemistry and Molecular Biology.
   D. Monograph Collection
      The Biochemistry Collection includes approximately 500 monograph volumes.
   E. Periodical Collection
      There are approximately 3000 volumes of periodicals in the collection.

4. JOHN CRERAR LIBRARY
   A. Name of Library
      The John Crerar Library
      35 West 33rd St.
      Chicago, Illinois 60616
   B. Name of Librarian
      William S. Budington, Executive Director and Librarian
   C. History and Development of the Collection
      No response.
   D. Monograph Collection
      Monographs were counted under the following call numbers:

547.81	581.105
547.9	591.105
575.16	612.015
576.34	618.92015
577.1	

      The total is approximately 3000 monographs.
   E. Periodical Collection

Periodicals listed under the same call numbers as above were counted, resulting in a total of approximately 160 serials.
F. Specially Noteable Features
The only noteable feature is the preponderance of medically related titles.

5. LIBRARY OF CONGRESS
   A. Name of Library
   Library of Congress
   Science and Technology Division
   10 First St. SE.
   Washington, D.C. 20540
   B. Name of Librarian
   John F. Price, Acting Chief Librarian
   The division has a staff of thirty-six people, more than half of whom are professionals with broad scientific and language competence.
   C. History and Development of the Collection
   The Library's biochemistry collections have been developed through the Library's regular acquisitions program and copyright deposits.
   D. Monograph Collection
   The size of the monograph collection is approximately 15,000 volumes. This figure was arrived at by counting the number of shelves under the call numbers listed, and then multiplying that number by thirty-six items per shelf.

   QD415-431
   QH345
   QH659
   QP501-801
   TP248.3

   E. Periodical Collection
   It is not possible to determine the size of the periodical collection. All bound journals are shelved with the monographs; this has most likely resulted in an overestimation of the number of monographs.

6. LOUISIANA STATE UNIVERSITY
   A. Name of Library
   Chemistry/Biochemistry Library

Branch of the Troy H. Middleton Library
Louisiana State University
Baton Rouge, Louisiana 70803
B. Name of Librarian
Bonita B. Brown, Chemistry Librarian
C. History and Development of the Collection
The Biochemistry Collection has historically been divided between the Troy H. Middleton Library and the Chemistry/Biochemistry Library. This holds true for both monographs and serials. There is only a small amount of duplication between the two libraries in the area of Biochemistry. Biochemistry books or journals are placed in one library or the other depending on which academic department requested the item. All Biochemistry Department requests are put into the Chemistry/Biochemistry Library. Requests from all other departments are placed in the Middleton Library even though they are in the subject area of Biochemistry.
D. Monograph Collection
The Biochemistry Collection has 2800 monograph volumes.
E. Periodical Collection
The Collection has 125 journal titles, 70 in the Middleton Library and 55 in the Chemistry/Biochemistry Library.

7. NATIONAL INSTITUTE OF ENVIRONMENTAL HEALTH SCIENCES
   A. Name of Library
      National Institute of Environmental Health Sciences
      Library and Information Services
      P.O. Box 12233
      Research Triangle Park, North Carolina 27709
   B. Name of Librarian
      W. Davenport Robertson, Head Librarian. There are are an additional six members to the library staff.
   C. History and Development of the Collection
      The Institute and the Library Collection began in about 1967. Serious collection building did not begin until 1977.
   D. Monograph Collection
      The total monograph collection is 4,000 volumes, of which about 1,500 are assignable to Library of Congress biochemistry classifications.
   E. Periodical Collection

There is a total of 500 journal subscriptions, 200–250 of which are in Biochemistry.

8. PUBLIC LIBRARY OF CINCINNATI AND HAMILTON COUNTY
   A. Name of library
      Public Library of Cincinnati and Hamilton County
      Science and Industry Department
      800 Vine Street
      Cincinnati, Ohio 45202
   B. Name of Librarian
      Rosemary Gaiser, Head, Science and Industry Department
   C. History and Development of the Collection
      The Science and Industry Department has a strong general collection in chemistry dating back many years. Although the Science and Industry Department does not have a special subject collection in any chemical area as such, all of the important subject fields in chemistry, including biochemistry, are represented. The emphasis is on American and British publications, but the collection also contains some German, French, and Canadian titles.
   D. Monograph Collection
      The chemical collection is in one location (the Science and Industry Department) and presently numbers approximately 14,000 volumes. Because Biochemistry is not treated as a separate collection, it is difficult to give the exact size of the Library's holdings in that field. A rough estimate of the volumes concerned strictly with biochemistry would be about 300, mostly general works.
   E. Periodical Collection
      The chemical periodical collection is also located in the Science and Industry Department. Approximately 200 titles are represented. The collection is especially strong in old periodicals. Outstanding abstracting journals include *Chemical Abstracts* (1907 to date), *Chemisches Zentralblatt* (1850 to 1949, with some gaps), and *British Abstracts* (1926–). The Library has complete files of *Beilsteins Handbuch der Organischen Chemie* as well as Landolt-Bornstein: *Zahlenwerte und Funtstronen aus Physik, Chemie, Astronomie, Geophysik und Technik*. Comprehensive periodical titles include Justus Liebig's *Annalen der Chemie* (1873 to date), *Angewandte Chemie* (1888–1961, 1962 to date), *Chemische Berichte* (1868 to date with some gaps), *Journal of the American*

Chemical Society (1879 to date), and *Canadian Chemical Processing* (1918 to date).
   F. Specially Noteable Features
   The Library has been a depository for the United States Government publications since 1884. The U.S. patent collection dates back to 1871. Holdings for British *Specifications of Inventions* are complete from 1884 to 1957, *Abridgements of Specifications* from 1617 to date.

9. UNIVERSITY OF ILLINOIS
   A. Name of Library
      Chemistry Library
      University of Illinois
      257 Noyes Lab
      Urbana, Illinois 61801
   B. Name of Librarian
      Lucille Wert, Chemistry Librarian
      Susanne Redalje, Assistant Chemistry Librarian
   C. History and Development of the Collection
      The collection has developed around the needs of the department. Currently, biochemistry is a department within the School of Chemical Sciences, which also includes chemistry and chemical engineering. Individual classes were taught in the area of biochemistry as early as the 1900s. The biggest advance came with the arrival of William Rose in 1922. Biochemistry first became a division within chemistry in 1953 and achieved its present status in 1969. An attempt is made to collect material sufficient for comprehensive research as well as to support the instructional needs of the students and faculty.
   D. Monograph Collection
      The biochemistry collection contains 950 monographic and serial titles, of which approximately 620 are monographs. The total number of volumes is 1,518. The primary collection is in the chemistry building, but is supplemented by the Biology Library on the campus. Access is also available, via daily shuttles, to the materials of the medical school in Chicago. Older volumes and editions are housed in the stacks of the main library.
   E. Periodical Collection
      The holdings include 153 journal titles, with approximately 6,055 volumes. As with monographs, there is some overlap with the

Biology Library and the Medical School. Many of the older volumes are in the stacks of the Main Library.
F. Specially Noteable Features
The main strength of the collection would be the long runs of many titles.

10. UNIVERSITY OF TEXAS AT AUSTIN
    A. Name of Library
       John W. Mallet Chemistry Library
       Welch Hall 2.132
       University of Texas
       Austin, Texas 78712
       The Science Library
       Main Building 220
       University of Texas
       Austin, Texas 78712
    B. Name of Librarian
       Assistant Director for Branch Services—Virginia Phillips
       Chemistry Librarian—A.E. Skinner
       Science Librarian—Betty J. White
    C. History and Development of the Collection
       Biochemistry as a research area began at Texas in 1939 with the addition of Dr. Roger J. Williams to the Chemistry faculty. In 1940, Dr. Williams founded the Biochemical Institute (later the Clayton Foundation Biochemical Institute) with the assistance of Mr. Benjamin Clayton of Houston, Texas. Mr. Clayton had a deep interest in cancer research and shared Dr. Williams' belief that advances in this field would come only as a result of studies of fundamental biochemical processes, sometimes seemingly unrelated to the cancer problem itself. Over the years, the Biochemical Institute has investigated such areas as the B vitamins; the composition, structure, and functioning of living cells; problems of differentiation; etiology of alcoholism; biochemical individuality; biochemical and molecular nutrition; and direct cancer research. Currently, the Institute has investigators dealing with such topics as protein crystallography; protein synthesis in eukaryotic cells; biochemical taxonomy and evolution of protein structure; protein biosynthesis; macromolecules of biological interest; metabolic antagonists and intermediate metabolism; structure, mechanisms of action, and regulation of organized enzyme systems; and nutri-

tional and biochemical approaches to prevention and therapy of diseases.

At present, the Clayton Foundation Biochemical Institute has eleven senior investigators and a total staff of approximately 100 persons.

Also active in biochemical research is the Institute for Biomedical Research, founded in 1968 by Dr. Karl Folkers, who holds a joint appointment in the Department of Chemistry and the College of Pharmacy. This Institute has a staff of some thirty-five persons, including about twenty post-doctoral scientists. Its overall thrust is multidisciplinary research in disease therapy, involving basic biochemical and biomedical studies, as well as companion clinical studies. The staff is a mix of organic chemists, biochemists, pharmacologists, biologists, physicians, and other health care professionals. Areas of research include coenzyme Q and vitamin B–6; and peptide hormones, especially those of the pituitary, hypothalamus, and thymus. The goal is new treatment of disease where there is no present or only ineffective treatment.

D. Monograph Collection

Biochemical materials at the University of Texas are shared between the Chemistry and Science Libraries. In determining the portions of each collection directly assignable to biochemistry, the following Dewey and Library of Congress classifications have been checked.

QP501–801	547.3–547.95
QD415–431.7	570 (relevant portions)
QH345	611–612 (relevant portions)
QK861–899	
QR467	

Using these as a guide, the shelf lists in each collection were checked, with the following results:

Chemistry Library: 2400 books assignable to the above numbers
Science Library: 3500 books assignable to the above numbers

E. Periodical Collection
Serials directly assignable to the above classification numbers:

Chemistry Library: 169 titles
Science Library: 186 titles

F. Specially Noteable Features
   The collection has been built over forty years to support research and teaching in what has become a major center of biochemical studies.

BOOK PUBLISHING IN BIOCHEMISTRY: VOLUME AND COSTS

Janice Sieburth

ABSTRACT. The *Publishers Trade List Annual (PTLA)* lists 1,425 biochemistry books published between 1975 and 1979. Twenty-five publishers produced 85.5 percent of these, with Academic Press and John Wiley the leaders. The figures showed 200 to 300 books added each year. The overall average price of a biochemistry book from one of the 25 major publishers was $34.00. The price is fairly steady at about $33.00 for books published in 1975–1978, but rose 12 percent to $38.00 in 1979. It appears that this rate of increase will continue. A comparison of various sources of information on book publishing shows that biochemistry books are about $10.00 more expensive than general medical or science books.

"It is more true in biochemistry than in most subjects that a book is bound to be out of date before it is published, but this does not deter biochemists from writing and reading them" (Rowland, 1974).

Books in any field of science provide a vehicle for the accumulation and synthesis of experimental research, an integration of older facts with new data, and a systematic presentation of a particular topic for review, teaching, and information exchange. This paper reports on a study of the volume of book publication and the range of average prices for books in the field of biochemistry. The five-year period from 1975 to 1979 was selected for surveying the major publishers and their production, and identifying any trends.

Scientific Book Production

In 1978, book sales in the United States totalled $5,772,000,000, including sales of $194,700,000 in medical books and $277,000,000 in technical and scientific books. These gross sales figures cover more than 1,200 book companies in the country, of which the ten largest generate

---

Janice Sieburth is Reference/Bibliographer and Assistant Professor, University of Rhode Island Library, Kingston, RI 02881.

twenty-five percent of the industry's revenue ("Communication, Publishing...", 1979). Overall sales figures are expected to rise at least ten percent in 1979 and again in 1980 (U.S. Department of Commerce, 1980).

The category of professional books which include medical, technical, scientific, and business today composes about 15 percent of the market, as compared with 11 percent ten years ago ("Communication, Publishing...", 1979). Revenues from this group reached $808,000,000 in 1978 (an increase of 15.2 percent over the previous year). Within this grouping, revenues from technical/scientific books were up 11.32 percent in 1978; from medical books, 19.2 percent.

Preliminary figures for publication volume in 1979 compiled by the R.R. Bowker Company show an output of 2,067 scientific books at an average price of $28.61, as compared with 1978 figures of 2,331 at $26.80. For medical books the output was 2,045 at $27.73 for 1979, as compared with 2,199 at $25.01 for 1978 (Grannis, 1980).

The literature on book production studies is scanty. Dessauer (1974) describes the increasing specialization of professional books and the shrinking market for them as the number of readers decreases. Orlov (1976) deplores the lack of hard data in most areas of publishing, especially any information on scholarly book production in particular fields. Chen (1977) lists major biomedical publishers and notes that there are four types of publishing concerns; trade publishers, university presses, learned or research societies and institutions, and government publishing offices. Her study also indicated that trade publishers were the major producers of biomedical books, supplying 88 percent of the total books available in the United States between 1970 and 1973.

Methodology

Publishers Trade List Annual was chosen as the source of an extensive listing of books currently in print. The six volumes for 1979 contain catalogs of publishers having a minimum listing of four pages and a section of those with shorter entries. A subject index compiled from information submitted by the publishers provided listings in the categories of medicine and dentistry, and science and technology. Although the author notes that the listing is not complete, it was used with the realization that it was the most comprehensive available.

This information from each of the publishers was scanned, title by title, for biochemistry books. The words in the title were used to indicate biological or biochemical interest, with a broad definition based on the article on "Biochemistry" in the *McGraw-Hill Encyclopedia of Science and Technology* (1977). Chemical work on living organisms; the study of substances such as proteins, nucleic acids, lipids, minerals, and enzymes; the metabolism of these compounds; nitrogen fixation and photosynthesis, and the chemical basis of disease were representative of the topics included. Books dealing primarily with microbiology, immunology, pathology, endocrinology, and similar subjects were not included unless the emphasis seemed to be on the chemical aspects of these fields of study.

A tabulation was made of the total number of titles of biochemical books for each publisher for the years 1975, 1976, 1977, 1978, and 1979, along with the listed price of each title. The total number of books for each year, the average price per year, the total for the five-year period, and the overall price were calculated. In a few cases where prices were not listed, the current *Books in Print,* 1979–1980, was used as a source of cost. There was no distinction made between imported and domestic products, nor among hardcover, softcover, or paperback. When there were several prices for different bindings, the hardcover or library binding price was used. It was intended that only new books or new editions be included, not reprintings. Several volume sets were counted as separate items.

To follow up and confirm the quantities and prices in the *Publishers Trade List Annual,* the *Subject Guide to Books in Print, 1979–1980* was checked under the listing for "Biological chemistry." All titles from this section were included which had an imprint indicated for one of the five years of study plus pertinent books from those sections indicated by "see also." These included: acid-base equilibrium, biochemical genetics, body composition, chemical genetics, chromatographic analysis, cytochemistry, enzymes, histochemistry, immunochemistry, metabolism, microbial metabolites, molecular biology, photosynthesis, physiological chemistry, and radioisotopes in biochemistry.

Results and Discussion

The 1979 edition of the *Publishers Trade List Annual (PTLA)* lists 1,346 publishers. Of these, 326 were represented in the catalogs section, which requires a minimum of four pages, and 1,020 in the yellow-paged supplement. Trade publishers, scientific societies, and university presses are included. Some entries list only one title, while other catalogs may run to several hundred pages.

The Subject Index to the publishers in the *PTLA* allowed the selection of publishers under headings for Medicine and Dentistry and under Science and Technology. The total number of these two groups, 302 publishers, were utilized for this study. Eighty-four were found in both lists; 142 were in the total medical, 244 in science.

Table 1 lists alphabetically the 65 publishers which were identified as

TABLE 1. Publishers listed in the <u>Publishers Trade List Annual</u>, the number of biochemistry books produced between 1975 and 1979, and the average cost per volume.

PUBLISHERS	NUMBER OF BOOKS	AVERAGE COST
Academic Press, Inc.	290	$35.97
Addison-Wesley Publishing Co.	12	20.44
Allyn and Bacon, Inc.	6	20.78
Annual Reviews	2	18.00
American Chemical Society	66	32.07
American Society for Microbiology	5	24.60
AVI Publishing Co., Inc.	21	28.45
Biomedical Publications	3	26.67
Bobbs-Merrill Co., Inc.	1	7.50
Cold Spring Harbor Laboratory	6	52.00
Colorado Associated University Press	1	1.95
Crane, Russak and Co., Inc.	2	43.50
F. A. Davis Co.	3	9.00
Walter de Gruyter, Inc.	10	93.69
Dowden, Hutchinson and Ross, Inc.	12	28.50
Drug Intelligence Publications	6	39.48
Eden Medical Research, Inc.	27	19.48
Edwards Brothers	1	38.00
M. Evans and Co., Inc.	1	8.95
W. H. Freeman	18	18.78
Gordon and Breach	3	14.95
Grune and Stratton	18	31.24
Harper and Row Publishing Co., Inc.	21	19.18
Harvard University Press	3	31.15
Holt, Rinehart and Winston, Inc.	3	16.13
Iowa State University Press	3	16.83
Johnny Reads, Inc.	1	35.00
S. Karger AG	82	59.14
William Kaufmann, Inc.	2	7.60
Robert E. Krieger Publishing Co.	6	24.08
Lange Medical Publications	2	11.25
Lea and Febiger	2	14.25
Lexington Books	2	17.48
Little, Brown and Company	9	17.92
McGraw-Hill Book Company	18	21.03
Macmillan Publishing Co., Inc.	16	14.71
Masson Publishing Co.	12	30.52
Merck and Co., Inc.	1	18.00
The MIT Press	11	13.71
Mojave Books	2	6.48
National Academy of Sciences	28	7.29
National Biomedical Research Foundation	3	46.33

TABLE 1. Continued

Publisher	Books	Avg. Cost
Nelson-Hall Inc.	3	14.95
Noyes Data Corporation	12	39.00
Pergamon Press, Inc.	106	38.54
Plenum Publishing Corp.	20	16.23
Raven Press	85	33.20
Rockefeller University Press	1	30.00
Rutgers Center of Alcohol Studies	2	7.00
SP Medical and Scientific Books	6	24.67
Springer Publishing Co., Inc.	1	48.50
Stratton Intercontinental Medical Book Corp.	10	17.87
Charles C. Thomas, Inc.	33	26.02
University of Alberta Press	1	6.95
University of California Press	2	37.50
University of Massachusetts Press	1	35.00
University of Pennsylvania Press	1	20.00
University of South Carolina Press	1	27.50
University of Texas Press	1	24.50
University Park Press	95	31.64
Urban and Schwarzenberg, Inc.	5	26.50
Van Nostrand Reinhold Co.	3	25.80
Vantage Press, Inc.	1	12.50
Verlag Chemie International Inc.	8	44.34
John Wiley and Sons, Inc.	186	36.94
Williams and Wilkins Co.	10	33.29
Yale University Press	1	15.00
Yorke Medical Books	2	19.50

TOTAL: 65 publishers

producing biochemical books. The total number of books found for each publisher with imprint dates of 1975 to 1979 is included, as well as the average cost of these volumes. Overall, 1,425 books are included in this list. The range of number of items for publishers varied from 1 to 290 and the average cost per volume from $1.95 to $93.69. Fifteen publishers with only one title listed were included.

The 25 largest publishers of biochemical books are included in Table 2 in quantitative order. Academic Press heads the list with 290 books; then Wiley, 186; Pergamon, 106; University Park Press, 95; Raven Press, 85; Karger, 82; and the American Chemical Society, 66. These six publishers represent 64 percent of the overall total, while the 25 publishers who produced 10 books or more represent 85.5 percent of the total. Fifteen of the 25 major publishers were included in both the medical and science lists in *PTLA*. The balance was divided between the two lists, with six only in the medical group and four only in the science list. The 25 major publishers included one university press, two scientific societies, and 22 trade publishers.

This could be compared with Chen's study of biomedical, scientific, and technical book reviewing in 1970 and 1973 (Chen, 1977), where it was found that 20 publishers produced 75 percent of the general biomedical books. It is interesting to note that the 10 top major biomedical trade publishers at that time were: Williams and Wilkins, Charles C. Thomas, Academic Press, Springer-Verlag, Appleton-Century Crofts, F.A. Davis, W.B. Saunders, Grune and Stratton, John Wiley, and C.V. Mosby. Of this list, Springer-Verlag, Appleton-Century Crofts, W.B. Saunders, and C.V. Mosby were not included in the 1979 *PTLA*. The other publishers are among the top 23 of this study, with Wiley and Academic in the top eight of both lists.

Publication volume of biochemistry books is available by year for all publishers of 10 or more titles in Table 3. The data seem to indicate that publishers are fairly consistent with the average prices charged from year to year.

Table 4 summarizes the data for production and price for the 25 major

TABLE 2. Major publishers of biochemistry books, listed in order by volume published with average price per volume.

PUBLISHER	NUMBER OF BOOKS	AVERAGE PRICE
Academic Press, Inc.	290	$35.97
John Wiley and Sons, Inc.	186	36.94
Pergamon Press, Inc.	106	38.54
University Park Press	95	31.64
Raven Press	85	33.20
S. Karger AG	82	59.14
American Chemical Society	66	32.07
Charles C. Thomas, Inc.	33	26.02
National Academy of Sciences	28	7.29
Eden Medical Research, Inc.	27	19.48
Harper and Row Publishing Co., Inc.	21	19.18
AVI Publishing Co., Inc.	21	28.45
Plenum Publishing Corp.	20	16.23
McGraw-Hill Book Company	18	21.03
Grune and Stratton	18	31.24
W. H. Freeman	18	18.78
Macmillan Publishing Co., Inc.	16	14.71
Noyes Data Corporation	12	39.00
Masson Publishing Co.	12	30.52
Dowden, Hutchinson and Ross, Inc.	12	28.50
Addison-Wesley Publishing Co.	12	20.44
MIT Press	11	13.71
Williams and Wilkins Co.	10	33.29
Walter de Gruyter, Inc.	10	93.69
Stratton Intercontinental Medical Book Corp.	10	17.87

publishers. There are 1,219 biochemistry books with 1975 to 1979 imprints available to the librarian or book buyer from the 25 major publishers listed in *PTLA*. Between 200 and 300 new books have been added each year. It should be noted that it is probable that the 1979 total is incomplete, recognizing the general lag in publication dates.

Publishers Weekly reports total numbers of volumes published each year from 18 months of Bowker's *Weekly Record*. Categories include science and medicine as defined by Dewey Decimal Classificaton. Table 5 summarizes these production and average price figures for hardcover books.

Although the volume output appears to be relatively constant in Table 5, 1977 and 1978 figures are slightly larger. This is also the trend in the *PTLA* figures in Table 4, which show biochemistry book production to have reached a peak of 309 volumes in 1978. These figures draw on different bases, but the trend is similar. Quantities derived from *Books in Print (BIP)* in Table 6 reflect a relatively steady production in the field, with counts of 126, 122, and 125 volumes listed for 1976, 1977, and 1978, respectively. The *BIP* publisher list is larger than *PTLA*, but the sampling is more restrictive, depending on the presence of the word biochemistry or a synonym in the title.

The larger the sample, the more meaningful should be the average prices. An overall average price for the 1,219 biochemistry books listed in *PTLA* was $34.00. Table 4 shows a reasonably constant price of $33.00 for the four years from 1975 to 1978, then an increase of 14.9 percent for 1979 to $38.69.

Table 7 presents a comparison of average prices collected from *PTLA, BIP,* the Bowker survey, and acquisitions at the University of Rhode Island Library. Prices calculated from *BIP* are slightly lower than the average in *PTLA* but show the same trend. While the study included all types of books (hardcover, softcover, paperback) listed in *PTLA* and *BIP,* the Bowker figures are for hardcover books and represent the larger areas of medicine and science. The University of Rhode Island acquisition figures are for the eight months from July to February, 1979–1980, and show the average list price of books processed under "Chemistry" and "Health Science" departmental codes. These books were acquired through both an approval plan and by individual orders and represent mostly hardcover volumes. Biochemistry books were included in both categories, but the average list price showed a much higher cost incurred for chemistry books—$7.50 more per volume—and a more comparable average for the health science grouping.

Price figures for the broader fields of scientific and medical books were considerably lower during this five-year period. Both categories averaged about $10.00 less than the cost determined for biochemistry books. Added to the differential is the fact that the Bowker figures are for hardcover books, while the *PTLA* prices include less expensive paperback and softcover books.

PTLA figures show a gradual price increase of about $3.00 between 1975 and 1978 and nearly $3.00 more between 1978 and 1979. This represents an increase of 12 percent from 1978 to 1979, and is comparable to the 13.4 percent increase noted for the costs of all hardcover books from 1978 to 1979 (Grannis, 1980).

TABLE 3. Part 1. Publishers of biochemistry books listed alphabetically with the number of items published each year from 1975 to 1979.

PUBLISHER	NUMBER OF ITEMS				
	1975	1976	1977	1978	1979
Academic Press	63	67	84	68	8
Addison-Wesley	4	2	3	2	1
Avi	3	5	5	7	1
American Chemical Society	8	18	25	8	7
Walter de Gruyter	3	-	3	3	1
Dowden, Hutchinson and Ross	2	3	7	-	-
Evan Medical Research Inc.	-	4	9	9	5
W. H. Freeman	3	5	2	3	5
Grune and Stratton	4	2	5	5	2
Harper and Row	4	3	5	7	2
Karger	-	1	25	34	22
McGraw-Hill	1	1	6	8	2
Macmillan	3	1	4	6	2
MIT Press	2	4	2	3	-
Masson	-	-	4	3	5
National Academy of Science	2	5	7	11	3
Noyes Data Corp.	2	2	3	2	3
Pergamon	14	24	19	19	30
Plenum	4	6	2	3	5
Raven Press	15	18	10	24	18
Stratton Intercontinental	5	4	1	-	-
C. C. Thomas	7	10	2	8	6
University Park Press	16	20	13	35	11
Wiley	35	42	44	40	25
Williams and Wilkins	1	3	4	1	1

TABLE 3. Part 2. Publishers of biochemistry books listed alphabetically with the average prices for the items published each year from 1975 to 1979.

PUBLISHER	AVERAGE PRICE				
	1975	1976	1977	1978	1979
Academic Press	$39.25	$35.63	$34.05	$35.93	$33.47
Addison-Wesley	18.98	27.00	23.00	20.23	5.95
Avi	29.83	25.90	33.80	27.79	15.00
American Chemical Society	32.97	29.57	32.13	40.06	28.14
Walter de Gruyter	78.53	--	97.25	99.17	112.00
Dowden, Hutchinson, and Ross	36.50	27.33	26.71	--	--
Evan Medical Research Inc.	--	19.00	17.56	18.89	24.40
W. H. Freeman	23.32	17.24	10.88	14.73	23.19
Grune and Stratton	31.44	25.38	30.80	36.20	25.38
Harper and Row	18.35	19.75	14.86	24.28	12.75
Karger	--	22.25	58.30	58.43	62.88
McGraw-Hill	16.50	18.50	28.66	17.21	16.98
Macmillan	21.65	14.50	12.73	12.85	13.95
MIT Press	20.00	7.71	15.00	16.67	--
Masson	--	--	26.25	35.75	30.80
National Academy of Science	10.63	7.15	7.54	7.27	4.83
Noyes Data Corp.	36.00	39.00	38.00	40.50	41.00
Pergamon	33.86	39.65	32.70	32.66	47.27
Plenum	14.21	13.02	11.45	26.13	17.66
Raven Press	29.90	34.11	33.00	33.88	34.25
Stratton Intercontinental	18.79	18.69	9.95	--	--
C. C. Thomas	20.93	26.68	22.88	25.13	33.13
University Park Press	31.62	35.80	33.19	28.92	30.90
Wiley	40.84	41.22	33.05	30.56	41.27
Williams and Wilkins	39.50	31.65	32.86	25.00	42.00

All prices show some increase between 1975 and 1979 but confirm the statement in the *Bowker Annual,* 1979 that the total hardcover volume price has remained "remarkably steady" (Alldredge, 1979). This may not continue to remain true, however, as publishers' costs rise. Thus, a comparison of prices of biochemistry books listed by Wiley in the 1979 *PTLA* and those of the books in their 1980 catalog showed another $3.00 increase in the average price from $36.94 to $40.42, or 9.4 percent.

TABLE 4. Total number of biochemistry books listed in *Publishers Trade List Annual* for 1975-1979 for the 25 major publishers.

YEAR	NUMBER OF BOOKS	AVERAGE PRICE
1975	201	$33.53
1976	250	32.72
1977	294	33.39
1978	309	33.51
1979	165	38.69
TOTAL	1,219	34.00

TABLE 5. Production and average prices of domestic and imported hardbound books in science and technology from *Publishers Weekly*.

YEAR	SCIENCE		MEDICINE	
	Volumes	Average Price	Volumes	Average Price
1975[1]	2,321	$22.81	1,722	$22.15
1976[2]	2,223	24.42	1,959	24.04
1977[2]	2,419	24.88	2,196	24.00
1978[2]	2,331	26.20	2,199	25.01
1979[3]	2,067	28.61	2,045	27.73

[1] "U.S. Book Industry Statistics," 1977.
[2] Grannis, 1979.
[3] Grannis, 1980.

TABLE 6. Total number of biochemistry books listed in *Subject Guide to Books in Print* for 1975-1979 by year, with average price for each year and the overall total and average price.

YEAR	NUMBER OF BOOKS	AVERAGE PRICE
1975	83	$29.40
1976	126	31.01
1977	122	31.53
1978	125	34.19
1979	93	36.08
TOTAL	549	
OVERALL AVERAGE PRICE		32.47

TABLE 7. Comparative average prices of science, medical and biochemistry books for 1975 to 1979 from various sources.

SOURCE	*Publishers Trade List Annual*, 1979	*Books in Print* 1979-1980
SUBJECT COVERAGE	Biochemistry	Biochemistry
1975	$33.53	$29.40
1976	32.72	31.01
1977	33.39	31.53
1978	33.51	34.19
1979	38.69	36.08

TABLE 7. Continued.

SOURCE	Bowker Survey (Table 5)		URI Library Acquisition 7/79-2/80	
SUBJECT COVERAGE	Science	Medicine	Chemistry	Bioscience
1975	$22.81	$22.15		
1976	24.42	24.04		
1977	24.88	24.00		
1978	26.20	25.01		
1979	28.61	27.73	$46.33(175)*	$34.54(418)*

*Number of titles used to compute average list price.

BIBLIOGRAPHY

Alldredge, Noreen G. and Atkinson, Hugh C. "Prices of U.S. and Foreign Published Material." *Bowker Annual*, 1979, 332–334.

Books in Print, 1979–1980. New York: R.R. Bowker, 1979.

Chen, Ching-Chih, *Scientific and Technical Information Sources*. Cambridge, MA: MIT Press, 1977.

"Communication, Publishing, Broadcasting, Advertising: Basic Analysis." *Standard and Poor's Industry Surveys*, November 29, 1979, C74.

Dessauer, John P. *Book Publishing; What It Is, What It Does*. New York: R.R. Bowker, 1974.

Grannis, Chandler B. "1979 Title Output and Average Prices, Preliminary Figures." *Publishers Weekly*, February 22, 1980, *217* (7), 54–58.

Grannis, Chandler B. "Updated Book Output Statistics 1978: Title Production, Average Prices." *Publishers Weekly,* September 3, 1979, *216* (10), 44–48.

Hu, A.S.L. "Biochemistry." *McGraw-Hill Encyclopedia of Science and Technology.* New York: McGraw-Hill, 1977.

Orlov, Ann. "Demythologizing Scholarly Publishing." In *Perspectives on Publishing* edited by Altbach, Philip G. and McVey, Sheila. Lexington, MA: Lexington Books, 1976.

Publishers Trade List Annual. New York: R.R. Bowker, 1979.

Rowland, J.F.B. "Biochemistry, Biophysics, and Molecular Biology." In L.T. Morton's *Use of Medical Literature.* London: Butterworths, 1974.

Shores, Cecelia L. "Average Price of Monographs, July 1979–February 1980." University of Rhode Island, Personal Communication, March 1980.

Subject Guide to Books in Print, 1979-80. New York: R.R. Bowker, 1979.

"U.S. Book Industry Statistics: Prices, Sales, Trends." *Publishers Weekly,* February 14, 1977; *211* (7), 52–56.

U.S. Department of Commerce. Industry and Trade Administration. *U.S. Industrial Outlook for 200 Industries with Projections for 1984.* Washington, DC: U.S. Government Printing Office, 1980.

Wiley, John and Sons, Inc. *1980 Catalog.*

COLLECTION DEVELOPMENT: MONOGRAPHS FOR BIOCHEMISTRY

Ann Knight Randall

ABSTRACT. General considerations in selection of monographs in scientific libraries are reviewed, with special attention to automated advances. Descriptive material is provided for general announcement services, book review media, and other library aids and sources of information.

Librarians managing collection development in the sciences seek to acquire books that meet present and future needs, using the criteria of (1) significant subject content; (2) currency; (3) authoritative authors; (4) a fit within the collection scope of the library; and (5) a fit within the expressed or anticipated needs of library users. In all scientific libraries, selection practices lean heavily toward serial literature. In the research library in biochemistry and in other sciences generally, only 15–20 percent of funds allocated to support any specific subject is used for monographs.

The literature on information use by scientists is relatively heavy. Crane (1972) surveyed this literature and pointed out that the scientist's information-seeking behavior is closely tied to his affiliations without a research area, as well as to the literature in that area. Part of this dependence on affiliation relates to the exponential growth in the literature, such as that reported for biochemistry in the last decade by Garfield (1979).

Whatever the reasons, scientific researchers seeking information often interact informally with colleagues, outside the network of libraries, card catalogs, indexes and abstracts, and computerized bibliographic systems. The information in which they are interested is communicated along a model chair of oral communication, preprint, technical reports, journal reports, indexes, bibliographies, monographs, treatises, reference books.

Ann Knight Randall is Assistant University Librarian, Brown University, Box I, Providence, RI 02912.

The monographic literature serves the need for cumulative reporting on scientific findings by organizing sizeable bodies of information on specific subject matter. Price (1976) indicates that at any time in the growth of a scientific field, a high proportion of the research which is cited refers to relatively recent work. Garfield's (1979) citation analysis study covering the biochemical literature, 1969-1977, notes that biochemists are citing a higher proportion of literature that is older than five years, and that biochemistry articles contain more references than was previously the case. One might wonder, in light of the above, about the relative citing of serial and monographic literature. Table 1 contrasts serial and book reference counts in the October 1979 *Trends in Biochemical Sciences: Reference Edition*. It is interesting to note that the serial (86%) and monographic (14%) citation figures correspond roughly to the approximate percentages given earlier for the fund allocations to serials and monographs in scientific libraries.

Libraries and Scientific Information

Cumulative information that researchers wish to review is provided through the library, although Ladendorf (1970) notes:

> When he is forced to go outside of his local work environment, he contacts... usually, as a last resort an appropriate library or information center... he always uses the first source which... will cost him the least effort to use... unfortunately the formal information system—specifically libraries or information centers—is usually considered to be an information source which requires a high degree of effort...

As for the uses, values, and limitations of books in the sciences, Malinowsky (1976) observes:

> In libraries, it is often considered fashionable to sneer at textbooks. Like most automatic derogations, this sneer is ill-advised. With rapid advances in science—the pace of advance seems to be increasing in geometric ratio—even treatises and monographs are neglecting to cover introductory material. The bewildered student, seeking to bring his understanding up to the current stage of investigation, has no recourse but to fall back on the older textbooks...

Table 1
Citations to Monographs and Serials in "Trends in Biochemical Sciences: Reference Edition".

Article	Total Citations	Monographs	Serials
1	24	3	21
2	22	0	22
3	18	3	15
4	31	0	31
5	26	1	25
6	24	3	21
7	19	2	17
8	21	3	18
9	8	0	8
10	34	7	27
11	20	0	20
12	32	0	32
13	19	7	12
14	39	9	30
15	29	2	27
16	9	0	9
17	5	3	2
18	30	1	29
19	22	7	15
20	39	3	36
21	25	1	24
22	31	4	27
23	21	3	18
24	20	1	19
25	9	0	9

Total Monograph and Serial Citations............................456
Total Monograph Citations...63
Total Serials Citations...393
Percentage of Monograph Citations..................................13.8
Percentage of Serial Citations.....................................86.2

Libraries will remain important in information-seeking behavior. Yet changing use patterns among researchers and rapid developments in technology will impact on library collections in the next century. Shrinking library budgets and space considerations encourage cooperative acquisitions programs and interlibrary networking in lieu of building massive collections. Foreign language materials, highly specialized series, expensive sets, and microform projects are among the resource types which institutions seek to share. Weber (1980) has forecasted eighteen conditions which will change library internal operations, several of which impact directly upon collection development:

—Many of the newer programs or materials or services in research libraries will provide important new dimensions to library services but they are almost always add-on rather than replacement programs;

—Given the vast array of scholarly informational needs, research libraries must maintain traditional activities while assuming the new capabilities afforded by networking. There will be books and computer-output microforms;

—The formats in which publications will be available will increase far beyond those that have been traditional; perhaps 5% of acquisitions will be of audio and visual formats and somewhere between 5 and 10% may be microformats;

—It remains the case that distinctive, extensive, developing and well organized materials on specific subjects will constitute the heart of the academic library.

Automated Advances

In the last quarter of the twentieth century, library information and retrieval activities have been enhanced by computer formats and micropublications. With respect to collection development of the secondary literature, many interesting questions are raised. Weber (1980), for example, predicts that secondary publications will decline.

The following automated advances impact on collection development of monographs in biochemistry:

1. Bibliographic data base—Access points are provided to the secondary literature through *Chemical Abstracts, Biological Abstracts, Medline, Science Citation Index,* and *Excerpta Medica.* Retrieval of monographic citations creates user demands for selection or interlibrary loan services.

2. Non-Bibliographic data bases—Factual and numerical data bases including handbooks and data compilations may be accessed online via data bases such as Toxline, Chemcon, etc., and this is a growing fact. Specific data items in these compilations may be accessed and manipulated with greater ease than afforded by the use of the manual format. As another example, the same thing is true of the Smithsonian Science Information Exchange (SSIE), which reports ongoing research projects of interest to biochemists and other scientists and facilitates scientific communication.

3. Library Networks—In this category, the most direct effect on the selection process by automated advances is seen in the use of shared cataloging information available from libraries. Thus, the selector may benefit from the use of the online version of National Library Medicine cataloging (CATLINE) or from Library of Congress MARC tapes available through Lockheed Dialog or through printed tools such as *Biblioscan*. One book dealer specializing in the library trade, BroDart, has mounted its holdings with the Bibliograhic Retrieval Services (BRS) to provide a data base called Books.

Library selectors may accomplish their pre-order searching for publications information rapidly through access to cataloging networks such as the Ohio College Library Consortium (OCLC), the Research Libraries Information Network (RLIN), the Washington Library Network (WLN), and the University of Toronto Library Automation System (UTLAS). It is also now possible for selectors who wish to acquire a list of new biochemical monographs published in the last few years to initiate a subject search through CATLINE, Books, or RLIN.

Selection Sources for Monographs in Biochemistry

The monographic literature is identified in many different sources which vary according to arrangement, frequency recency, amount of identifying detail provided, geographic and language scope, annotation of subject content, and reliability of source.

A. General Announcement Services

The general announcement services included below cover English language publications primarily, with the exception of foreign titles cataloged by the National Library of Medicine or the Library of Congress.

1. American Book Publishers Record. R.R. Bowker Co. This biweekly publication is based upon the Weekly Record (see below). Titles appear in classifications arrangement according to the Dewey Decimal Classification. Most biochemical titles are listed under 574.19, although titles of interest may be classified in chemistry or clinical medicine (616).

2. *ASLIB Booklist.* London. This is a monthly list of selected books published in the fields of science, technology, medicine, and social sciences. The titles are arranged in classified order according to the Universal Decimal Classification. Classes 57, "Biological Sciences," and 61, "Medical Sciences," are germane. Entries provided descriptive annotations and audience level, such as A, elementary; B, intermediate; C, Advanced; and D, Reference book or practitioner manual. Prices are frequently provided.

3. *Biblioscan Q-Z.* Inforonics, INc. Wellesley Hills, Massachusetts. This monthly list of all new English language titles cataloged by the Library of Congress in Sciences, Medicine, and Technology is arranged in LC classification order and provides complete bibliographic information for each entry.

4. *Choice.* American Library Association. Association of College and Research Libraries. Middletown, Connecticut. This monthly publication, available both in serial form and in 3×5 cards, provides book reviews prepared by faculty reviewers. The descriptive and evaluative reviews indicate scope and type of library for which the items is recommended, and are often a good source for interdisciplinary titles not easily identified in the more specialized sources.

5. *Library of Congress Proof Slips.* Washington, D. C. Full classification information is available in 3×5 Library of Congress format, for all materials cataloged, including foreign language titles. Cards may be sorted and distributed to selectors, arranged by subject assignment.

6. *Current Catalog Proof Sheets.* National Library of Medicine. These provide alphabetical access to monographic and serial literature acquired for the Library's collection. Weekly issues supplement the bound catalog which is cumulated annually. Full bibliographic information, plus the NLM classification number, is provided. Price information is rarely available in this key announcement source for clinical biochemistry.

7. *New Technical Books.* The New York Public Library. Research Libraries. This selective list has descriptive annotations. Published

monthly, except August and September, and covering English language books, it is arranged by Dewey Decimal Classification.

8. *Weekly Record.* R.R. Bowker Co. This is a comprehensive and up-to-date alphabetical list of books published in English language covering all subjects. Dewey and Library of Congress classification is provided, along with full author, title, price, and series information when available. The inconvenience of searching all titles is offset by the timeliness of the information.

B. Book Review Media

Book reviews are especially beneficial when acquisitions dollars are limited, and the library is motivated to build a carefully selected, representative collection. They provide descriptive information and commentary from experienced selectors or researchers with advanced subject knowledge. These helpful factors must be balanced against the time lag between book publication and the printed review, which may range from six to eighteen months or longer. Most libraries will want to select useful monographs as soon as they are identified, and use reviews as a useful check on the selection process.

Chen (1976) has reported that 54 out of 285 life sciences English language journals, excluding *Science* and *Nature,* contained book reviews. The key biomedical reviewing journals identified by her study were: *British Medical Journal, Lancet, Annals of Internal Medicine, Journal of the American Medical Association, Archives of Internal Medicine, New England Journal of Medicine, Quarterly Review of Biology, Bioscience, Canadian Medical Association Journal,* and *American Journal of the Medical Sciences.* These accounted for 63% of the 3,347 reviews identified.

In addition to these high-yield journals, the following titles provide useful selection information: *American Scientist, American Journal of Physiology, Journal of the American Chemical Society, Journal of Medicinal Chemistry, Journal of Neurology, Neurosurgery and Psychiatry, Nature, Science,* and *Trends in Biochemical Sciences.* Books received are listed in many other biomedical journals which may serve an announcement function for the titles selected. Biomedical books are also listed or reviewed in library science publications such as the *Bulletin of the Medical Library Association* and *Library Journal.*

If the library has an approval plan, there may be less motivation for scanning announcement sources and review journals on a current basis. The approval agreement with the vendor specifies that monographs from the publishers, or those covering the subject scope specified, will be supplied automatically, subject to selector examination and a small percentage of returned titles.

Indexing and abstracting sources which provide access to book reviews include *Book Review Digest, Book Review Index, Index to Book Review Citations,* and *Technical Book Review Index.* A new publication (1980) from the Institute of Scientific Information, *Index to Book Reviews in the Sciences,* in a multidisciplinary index covering the life sciences, clinical medicine, physical sciences, chemical sciences, agriculture, engineering, and technology. ISI indicates that it covers over 3,000 scientific and technical journals and 140 behavioral sciences journals. Full index citations are provided to primary author or editor, title, publisher, price, reviewer, publication date, and journal in which the review appeared. The language of the book and the review are shown if other than English. Alphabetical access to significant works in the title is also provided.

C. Other Library Aids and Sources of Information

General announcement services and the book review media facilitate systematic selection on a current basis. The librarian selector will have access to additional library aids and other sources of information, such as core lists, gifts, interlibrary loan requests, patron recommendations, collection development policy, network and consortium holdings, publishers' brochures and advertisements, reference questions, book jobber and approval plan lists, and automated literature searches.

It should be noted that library collection development policies are rarely written and kept up to date. Within the last five years, many large libraries have given priority to producing a document that would describe existing collections and current levels of collecting within the various disciplines covered. A written policy is especially useful to selectors when it specifies the research areas where agreement exists that efforts will be made to acquire all significant monographic literature in order to support the institutional emphasis. By contrast, the minimal or basic areas would be represented by selected reference works and monographs suitable to cover general concepts at an introductory level. The policy is a plan of action, and it is also a public relations tool which will describe the collection to users and other libraries. The written policy facilitates cooperation because all parties to the agreement have a basis for expecting subject strength and weaknesses.

REFERENCES

Chen, Ching-Chih. *Biomedical Scientific and Technical Book Reviewing*. Metuchen, New Jersey: Scarecrow Press, 1976.

Crane, D. *Invisible Colleges: Diffusion of Knowledge in Scientific Communities*. Chicago; University of Chicago Press, 1972.

Garfield, Eugene. "Trends in Biochemical Literature." *Trends in Biochemical Sciences*, 1979, *4*, 290-5.

Ladendorf, Janice M. "Information Flow in Science, Technology and Commerce: A Review of the Concepts of the Sixties." *Special Libraries*, 1970, *61*, 215-222.

Price, D. J. D. "A General Theory of Bibliometric and Other Cumulative Advantage Processes." *Journal of the American Society of Information Science*, 1976, *27*, 292-306.

Malinowsky, H. Robert, and others. *Science and Engineering Literature: A Guide to Reference Sources*. Littleton, Colorado; Libraries Unlimited, 1976, p. 38.

Trends in Biochemical Sciences: Reference Edition, 1979, *4*, 217-291.

Weber, David C. "The Next fifty Years in Academic Libraries." *Oklahoma Librarian*, 1980, *30*, 26-31.

COLLECTION DEVELOPMENT: JOURNALS FOR BIOCHEMISTS

Tony Stankus

ABSTRACT. The types of serials of interest to biochemists are reviewed, as are the schools of science journal collection development. Results of pilot studies are presented: where American biochemists publish; authorship of articles in selected journals; publication patterns of authors in for-profit firms and in small liberal art colleges; journals most frequently cited in widely used biochemistry texts. A list of journals discussed is included.

Introduction

In addition to the intellectual curiosity involved, the study of serial collection development for biochemists is worthwhile because of the cost and complexity of the materials involved. The decision to add or cancel a single subscription may involve several hundred dollars and comparison of numerous titles. To compound the problem, publication in biochemistry is growing at a rapid rate. Garfield (1979) reports three journals which published more than a thousand papers in 1977 (one of them exceeded two thousand papers) and estimates the total production of papers in that year as 20–25,000. Virtually every library with a substantive collection in the life sciences will have biochemistry serials and should have a policy for their selection.

Historical Background

The development of the serial literature in biochemistry has been discussed by Sengupta (1973). Between the late 1800s and the First World War, the French, Germans, Americans, and British established

---

Tony Stankus is Science Librarian, Science Library, College of the Holy Cross, Worcester, MA 01610. The author wishes to thank the New England area biochemists and biochemical publishing representative with whom he consulted, particularly Dr. Peter Parsons, Holy Cross College, and Dr. Mary Lee Ledbetter, Dartmouth Medical School. He would also like to thank the editor, Dr. Bernard S. Schlessinger, for his invaluable assistance in the final preparation of this paper.

scientific societies devoted to better understanding the relationship between chemistry and living organisms. These national societies sponsored journals to publish in their native languages the results of specifically biochemical work. These include, respectively, *Biochimie, Hoppe-Seylers Zeitschrift fuer Physiologische Chemie,* the *Journal of Biological Chemistry,* and the *Biochemical Journal.* These journals gave increased visibility and respectability to the field and, gradually at first, drew biochemically oriented manuscripts away from the neighboring disciplines of general and organic chemistry, microbiology, and physiology. After the Second World War, the science publishing world exploded with many new biochemistry journals, some no longer directly sponsored by a scientific society and most dominated by English-language articles. Some of the more alert journals of neighboring disciplines sought to hold on to their biochemically concerned readers and have increasingly featured papers using biochemical methods. This time of rising status for biochemistry also saw increased acceptance of biochemistry papers in the prestigious multiscience journals. As a consequence of these trends, Sengupta too sees more and more biochemistry papers in more and more kinds of journals, although he sees the more specifically biochemical journals as most important.

Types of Serials for Biochemists

Serials for biochemists may be classified in at least two ways: (1) by the function and/or length of the papers ordinarily published and (2) by the subject orientation of the papers ordinarily published.

In the function/length category, several subclasses of journals are found.

1. A journal that publishes primarily the results of original research in longer articles with structural elements such as abstracts, introductions, experimental details, results, and discussions may be referred to as a FULL-LENGTH ORIGINAL REPORTS JOURNAL. Examples include the *Journal of Biological Chemistry* and *Biochemistry.* Publishing in one of these journals is prestigious, in part because of the very rigorous examination of a given paper's worth by a somewhat lengthier refereeing process.

2. The delay between submission and appearance of articles in Full-Length Original Reports Journals (due to the lengthier refereeing procedures and the large numbers of papers chronically backlogged) and the

fact that not all studies lend themselves to this format have led to the development of the RAPID, PRELIMINARY COMMUNICATIONS (or "LETTERS") JOURNAL. The studies reported in these journals are in the form of shorter papers, often reporting preliminary results. Newsworthiness is stressed; the format is not as structured. Referees are instructed to quickly assess submitted papers and to make reasonable allowance for very new or speculative interpretation in the interests of rapid dissemination. *Biochemical and Biophysical Research Communications* is an example of all of these characteristics, while *FEBS Letters* stresses a more conclusive finding with equal brevity and speed of processing.

3. The desire for speed and priority of announcement, especially of reports presented at meetings, has resulted in appearance of the MEETING ABSTRACT JOURNAL or the MEETING ABSTRACT SPECIAL ISSUES (of either a full-length or rapid preliminary communications journal). In these journals, presenters scheduled for meetings publish paragraph-sized summaries of their presentations. The journals usually appear in print well before the conference. Examples of these journals are found in the special issues of the *Biophysical Journal* and the *Journal of Supramolecular Structure*.

4. Biochemists have felt a neccessity to grasp the central themes and generalizing theories of their profession. They have recognized that one is in danger of seeing only the thousands of trees (full-length articles; rapid, preliminary communications; meetings abstracts) and failing to comprehend the totality of the forest. For this reason, the REVIEW SERIAL was born. In Review Serials, authors present long essays which summarize and classify the main channels of work in a given specialty by discussing a great many papers written over a given time span. The physical appearance of the type of review serial defined here is usually hardbound, and issuance is often irregular. A well-known hardbound series is the *Annual Review of Biochemistry;* a familiar softbound is the *CRC Critical Reviews in Biochemistry*.

In the subject-orientation category, six subclasses are also present, divided into two classes of specialty journals in biochemistry and four classes of more general journals or journals in other disciplines of importance to biochemists.

The first class of specialty journals is devoted to classes of biochemical substances. SUBSTANCE SPECIALTY JOURNALS vary in format from the full-length *Journal of Lipid Research* to the rapid-communication-like *Nucleic Acids Research* to the evaluative essays in *Advances in Protein Chemistry*.

The second class of SUBSPECIALTY JOURNALS deal with a central theme or phenomena, a class of organism, a methods approach, or with an applied biochemistry field. Examples include, respectively, the *Journal of Immunology, Insect Biochemistry, Analytical Biochemistry,* and *Clinical Chemistry*.

In the more general or other-disipline journals can be found:

1. the MISSION-ORIENTED JOURNALS. The contents focus on a societal or medical problem. Examples are *Cancer Research* and the *Biology of Reproduction*.

2. the MULTISCIENCE JOURNALS. Both original and review papers in biochemistry and many other sciences are published here. A mix of short, newsworthy rapid communications and extended, authoritative reviews dominate in journals such as *Science* and *Nature,* while a medium-length paper dominates journals such as the *Proceedings of the National Academy of Sciences*.

3. the HYBRIDIZED JOURNALS. These attract the biochemically oriented researchers in other disciplines to publish with biochemists in one common journal at the mutual border of the two disciplines. Examples include *Biochemical Genetics, Biochemical Medicine,* and *Biochemical Pharmacology*.

4. the NEIGHBORING DISCIPLINE JOURNALS. The journals in biochemistry, as noted earlier, took their content from journals in fields such as microbiology, medicine and chemistry. Biochemists still publish within and cite these journals. Prominent examples include the *Journal of Bacteriology,* the *Journal of Clinical Investigation,* and the *Journal of the American Chemical Society*.

Current Schools of Science Journal Collection Development

There are two current schools of thought on how librarians select from among the wide variety of journals described above for their scientific journals collection. Each of these schools may be said to have its own principal tool.

The first school of thought focuses on the sponsorship of the journal and its publication in English. The importance of selecting English-language journals published by well-known societies is reflected in the lists of periodicals in the common science literature texts (Chen, 1975; Malinowsky, 1976; Mount, 1975). The frankest statement of this school of thought can be found in what is probably the most widely consulted library journals selection tool, *Magazines for Libraries* (Katz & Richards, 1978): "Titles have been slected to include the main English-language research journals sponsored by distinguished societies in the United States, Canada, and Great Britain (and) some high quality commercial publications commonly found in academic/special libraries."

What is not clear is to what degree this "Society Sponsorship & English-Language Publication" rule is to be applied when selecting journals from non-English-speaking countries. For example, Stankus, Schlessinger, and Schlessinger (1981) have shown that a large number of basic science journals, both society sponsored and commercial, based in Germany and formerly publishing in German, are now publishing the vast majority of their material in English. Katz and Richards endorse many of them and thereby seem to be extending their rule, at least in the cases of the society-sponsored titles. But this still leaves us with the problems of many commercial titles and with those foreign-language journals with a society sponsorship. The librarian cannot expect a resolution in Katz and Richards, for they note that they cannot list ever good journal and that *Magazines for Libraries* serves many libraries for whom the price of the commercial journals and the difficulties of comprehension of foreign-language material by patrons would argue against selection.

One help for selection of foreign-language journals is afforded by the second school of thought about scientific journal selection, the citation analysis approach (Garfield, 1972, 1976). This approach is based on the cumulative citation behavior of tens of thousands of scientists as they publish their papers and cite their own work and that of others. A basic assumption of citation analysis is that the scientific community within a given discipline will, over the long run, cite the better works in the better journals more often, and that the citation count can serve as an indicator of the importance of a journal. That librarians should select journals with articles heavily cited, in the disciplines they work with seems reasonable, since citation frequency should correlate with user demand. (Stankus and Rice, 1981).

In actual operation, the use of citation data in scientific journal selection would require that the librarian screen a list of journals in citation frequency order and select those pertinent journals at the top of the list. Such lists exist in *JCR (Journal Citation Reports)* (Garfield, 1975). The lists of "most cited," "highest impact," "immediacy indexes," etc. and the individual analyses of specific journals gain in validity with comparisons made using several years' data.

The *JCR* and its parent *Science Citation Index* data base have been the source for much literature evaluating journals in given fields, including some dealing with biochemistry. In one recent study, Garfield (1979) closely analyzes the citation behavior of 40 biochemical journals, those "core" journals which publish exclusively papers in biochemistry. Two tables in the article list journals of all types ranked by the frequency with which they cite, or are cited by, these "core" biochemistry journals. Many of these "core" journals are on both lists, an expected tight interaction. The lists also contain surprisingly many multiscience, mission-oriented, hybridized, and neighboring discipline journals. (All journals from either of the lists, and any others mentioned in this paper, are listed in Appendix I.) This citation analysis approach also poses some questions, for example:

1. Should the librarians select the more narrowly defined biochemistry "core" journals as a general rule?
2. Or, should the librarians select, within funding limits, any journals that cite or are cited by biochemists?
3. Is a special collection for biochemists better served with its own subscriptions to American journals like *Cell*, the *Journal of Bacteriology*, and the *Journal of Clinical Investigation* rather than to foreign journals like the *Journal of Biochemistry (Tokyo)*, *Hoppe-Seyler's Zeitschrift fuer Physiologische Chemie*, or *Biochimie?*

Many other questions can be posed. They lead to the conclusion that the works of Garfield warrant analysis and sophistication on the part of working librarians before casual attempts at application.

On final point should be made on the use of citation analysis. The Garfield data is all-inclusive in its audience. It speaks to scientists and librarians, to foreign as well as to American audiences. When, for example, the data show that the *Journal of Biochemistry (Tokyo)* is the 16th most-cited journal of any kind among the core journals of biochemistry, that statement is made on the basis of inclusion of all citations made by the Japanese within that journal (and any others within which they publish) as well as the more occasional American references to it. (The same statement may be made for journals published by the Germans, French, etc.) Garfield has explored the citation behavior of certain foreign groups of journals (Garfield, 1977), but largely with the view of persuading them to increase their use of English by demonstrating the "under-citedness" of articles and journals written in languages other than English. What American librarians need is some indication of specific American involvement, possibly through study of citation made by Americans. This has not yet been done but may one day be available.

Other Tools for Selection

The two schools noted above can be helpful in decisions of collection development. One other possible tool rests upon an analysis of where specifically American biochemists publish. This type of study has been approached in the following pilot investigation by the author. A sample of American institutions or departments likely to publish regularly in biochemistry journals was identified in four different categories: Medical Schools, Universities, Federal Establishments, and independent Research Foundations. Using recent issues of the "Corporate Index" of *Science Citation Index* for a period of time long enough to avoid peaks and valleys in publication, the output of the various units was tabulated, with the intent of identifying for each group over a three-year span 25-30 journals in which some group members published each year. Table 1 presents the results for 40 institutions and departments (the specific locations are included in Appendix 2). It can be seen that society-sponsored journals published in English do well, as for example, *Journal of Biological Chemistry, Biochemistry,* and *Biochemical Journal.* It may also be observed that every journal on the list in Table 1 is very highly cited, and, in fact, all 12 of the "core" biochemistry journals on the Garfield list of the top 100 journals of any disciplines also appear on this list. Other observations are worth making:

1. Only a handful of foreign-editorially-based journals appear on any of the lists. These include *Nature;* the *Journal of Molecular Biology; Biochemical Journal; Biochimical et Biophysica Acta;* and the *European Journal of Biochemistry.*

2. Despite the fact that they accept English-language papers, neither *Biochimie; Hoppe-Seylers Zeitschrift . . . ;* the *Journal of Biochemistry (Tokyo),* nor any Eastern Bloc journals appear on the list. American librarians must consider whether they can afford to spend hundreds of dollars annually on these and other "bridesmaid journals" (i.e., journals that the librarian's research customers might only cite from time to time) in contrast to "bride journals" (i.e., journals that these customers not only cite but publish in).

3. There is a strong presence of the multiscience, hybridized, and neighboring-discipline journals. It appears that for Americans these

Table 1. Journals Published in by American Biochemists Working in Specific Areas, 1977-1979

Part 1. Medical Schools and Universities

Medical Schools			Universities	
1.	J. Biol. Chem.	238	Biochemistry	196
2.	Proc. Nat. Acad. Sci.	96	J. Biol. Chem.	179
3.	Biochemistry	86	Proc. Nat. Acad. Sci.	155
4.	Biochim. Biophys. Acta	46	Cell	83
5.	Fed. Proc.	42	J. Bacteriol.	72
6.	Cell	32	J. Mol. Biol.	56
7.	Anal. Biochem.	29	Biochem. Biophys. Res. Commun.	54
8.	Biochem. Biophys. Res. Commun.	28	Biochim. Biophys. Acta	44
9.	J. Bacteriol.	23	Nature	44
10.	Arch. Biochem. Biophys.	22	Nucleic Acid Res.	44
11.	J. Cell Biol.	21	J. Cell Biol.	36
12.	Nature	17	Arch. Biochem. Biophys.	33
13.	Nucleic Acid Res.	16	Virol.	33
14.	FEBS Letters	16	J. Virol.	30
15.	J. Mol. Biol.	15	Science	28
16.	J. Immunol.	15	Anal. Biochem.	27
17.	Endocrinology	14	J. Am. Chem. Soc.	26
18.	J. Clin. Invest.	13	Biopolymers	21
19.	Science	13	Mol. Gen. Genet.	17
20.	Carbohydrate Res.	12	Cold Spring Harbor Symp. Quant. Biol.	13
21.	Biochem. J.	11	J. Immunol.	12
22.	Mol. Pharmacol.	11	FEBS Letters	12
23.	Pediatric Res.	10	J. Cell Physiol.	12
24.	Biochem. Pharmacol.	9	Cancer Res.	8
25.	Exp. Cell Res.	9	Exp. Cell Res.	7
26.	J. Supramol. Struct.	9	Phytochem.	6
27.	Eur. J. Biochem.	7	J. Neurochem.	5
28.	Annu. Rev. Biochem.	7	Biochem. Genet.	4

28 journals produced 629 articles of 116 journals producing 794 articles

28 journals produced 1257 articles of 100 journals producing 1428 articles

Note: Three meetings abstracts equal one paper.

Table 1. (cont.)

Part 2. Independent, Non-Profit Research Foundations and Federal, Veterans and Military

Independent, Non-Profit Research Foundations			Federal, Veterans and Military	
1.	Proc. Nat. Acad. Sci.	67	J. Biol. Chem.	57
2.	Biochem. Biophys. Res. Commun.	44	Proc. Nat. Acad. Sci.	40
3.	Fed. Proc.	40	Biochemistry	28
4.	J. Biol. Chem.	38	Clin. Chem.	27
5.	Nature	37	J. Cell Biol.	17
6.	J. Virol.	36	Biochem. Biophys. Res. Commun.	16
7.	Endocrinology	35	Cell	16
8.	Biochim. Biophys. Acta	33	J. Immunol.	13
9.	Biochemistry	27	J. Virol.	12
10.	Cell	27	Fed. Proc.	11
11.	J. Nat. Cancer Inst.	24	J. Mol. Biol.	11
12.	Cancer Res.	24	Science	11
13.	J. Cell Physiol.	22	Nature	11
14.	Proc. Amer. Assoc. Cancer Res.	19	J. Gen. Virol.	10
15.	Biol. Reprod.	19	Anal. Biochem.	10
16.	Science	18	Biochim. Biophys. Acta	10
17.	Virology	16	J. Chromatography	9
18.	Life Sci.	16	Arch. Biochem. Biophys.	9
19.	Biochem. Pharmacol.	14	Cancer Res.	7
20.	Exp. Cell Res.	13	Clin. Res.	7
21.	J. Immunol.	12	J. Cell Physiol.	7
22.	J. Mol. Evol.	11	J. Supramol. Struct.	6
23.	J. Exp. Med.	11	Mol. Pharmacol.	6
24.	Biophys. J.	8	FEBS Letters	4
25.	J. Mol. Biol.	8		
26.	J. Gen. Virol.	6		
27.	Cytogenet. Cell Genet.	6		
28.	Mol. Pharm.	4		

28 journals produced 635 articles of 177 journals producing 908 articles

24 journals produced 363 articles of 106 journals producing 599 articles

Note: Three meetings abstracts equal one paper.

related journals have equal status to most "core" biochemistry titles with the exceptions of the most highly regarded *Journal of Biological Chemistry* and *Biochemistry*. It should be further noted, however, that Americans do appear to choose only the more-cited of these related journals in which to publish, eg., *Cell* or the *Journal of Cell Biology*, rather than *Cytobios*.

As a further investigation, the author analyzed the authorship (U.S. vs. others) in articles in some of the journals in question. The most recent year available at the time of this study, 1978, was chosen for analysis and samples used, of no less than 50% (excepting for 25% for the titanic *Biochimica et Biophysica Acta*) of the total publication in that year. The results are shown in Table 2. Analysis of the results indicates that:

1. Generally, Americans publish in journals controlled by U.S. editors, foreign authors in journals controlled by editors of similar persuasion.
2. A "critical mass" for publication by Americans in foreign journals seems to be about 100 American papers per year. It would seem that publication by American authors in foreign journals is effectively a socialization phenomenon and is based on knowing that a reputable American colleague or research group has published there.

The author also analyzed publication practices of authors in for-profit firms and in small liberal arts colleges.

In the case of for-profit firms, the directory *Industrial Research Laboratories of the U.S.* (Cattell Press, 1970) was used to develop a list of for-profit institutions that were biochemistry oriented. Analysis of three years of the Corporate Index of *Science Citation Index* produced some indications of industry-by-industry patterns. It would appear that:

1. Authors in pharmaceutical firms regularly publish in the hybridized *Biochemical Pharmacology, Molecular Pharmacology*, and the rapid preliminary communications journal *Life Sciences*.
2. Authors in biochemical and clinical laboratory supply firms publish heavily in *Clinical Chemistry* and less frequently in *Clinica Chimica Acta, Clinical Biochemistry*, and the *Journal of Laboratory and Clinical Medicine*.
3. Authors in firms dealing with food and agricultural products

Table 2. Geographic Affiliation of Authors in Journals of Biochemical Interest

Journal	Editorial Control U.S.	Editorial Control Foreign	Number and (%) of Papers U.S.	Number and (%) of Papers Foreign	Number of Papers and (%) of Annual Output in Sample
J. Biol. Chem.*	X		686(83)	142(17)	828(57)
Biochem. Biophys. Res. Comm.*	X		547(53)	479(47)	1026(100)
Science*(B)	X		100(92)	14(8)	114(100)
Biochemistry*	X		415(83)	89(17)	504(57)
Proc. Nat. Acad. Sci.*(B)	X		252(77)	75(23)	327(70)
Arch. Biochem. Biophys.*	X		271(75)	99(25)	370(100)
Anal. Biochem.*	X		284(60)	172(40)	456(100)
J. Mol. Biol.*		X	172(54)	151(46)	323(100)
Nature*(B)		X	171(52)	156(48)	327(50)
Biochim. Biophys. Acta*		X	301(38)	509(62)	810(25)
Biochem. J.*		X	101(16)	492(84)	593(65)
FEBS Letters*		X	104(13)	681(87)	785(80)
Eur.J.Biochem.*		X	70(9)	700(91)	770(100)
Experientia(B)		X	56(25)	171(75)	227(100)
Int.J.Biochem.		X	39(28)	101(72)	140(100)
Mol.Cell Biochem.		X	27(40)	40(60)	67(100)
Biochimie		X	13(8)	150(92)	163(100)
Can. J. Biochem.		X	9(6)	153(94)	162(100)
Naturwissensch.(B)		X	8(29)	20(71)	28(100)
J.Biochem.(Tokyo)		X	6(3)	245(97)	351(100)
Hoppe-Seyler's Z.		X	2(1)	177(99)	179(100)
Biochemistry(USSR)		X	0(0)	239(100)	239(100)
			3624	5155	8779

*Journals Containing a "Critical Mass" of American Papers

(B) Only Biochemistry papers counted in this multiscience journal

U.S. papers in journals with "Critical Mass" = 3474
U.S. papers in journals without "Critical Mass" = 150

publish in the *Journal of Food Science:* the *Journal of Agricultural and Food Chemistry:* the class of biochemical substance specialty journals (the *Journal of the American Oil Chemists Society* and *Cereal Chemistry*), and three kinds of neighboring discipline journals (the *Journal of Nutrition, Plant Physiology,* and the *Journal of the Association of Official Analytical Chemists.*).

4. Authors in laboratories involved with cancer screening and product safety favor *Food and Cosmetic Toxicology* and *Toxicology and Applied Pharmacology* and in particular announce their findings in a Meeting Abstracts special issue (*Proceedings of the American Association for Cancer Research*) of *Cancer Research*.

5. Authors working in the new area of genetic engineering have appeared in *Nature* and *Science*, as well as in the *Proceedings of the National Academy of Sciences, Journal of Biological Chemistry, Journal of Molecular Biology, Journal of Bacteriology*, and the virological journals. *Molecular and General Genetics* and *Gene* appear to be oriented toward these authors.

For investigating the publication habits of the liberal-arts-college biochemists, a group of eighty schools was identified (Cass, 1978) and publication patterns developed, using the Corporate Index of the *Science Citation Index* for the periods 1965–71 and 1972–78. the results are shown in Table 3. Analysis of the results show that:

1. While the preferential order of the biochemistry journals is altered, many of the same journals are on this list as well as on those lists developed earlier earlier.

2. The *Journal of Biological Chemistry* and *Biochemistry* do not dominate as they do on other lists. This is probably due to the comprehensive, full-length, and conclusive nature of papers accepted by these journals. Most research in liberal-arts colleges is limited. This also probably explains the favored position of *Biochemical Biophysical Research Communications* (which specializes in more preliminary and shorter works for these authors.). The popularity of *Comparative Biochemistry and Physiology* may be explained in that instructors at some of these smaller institutions are hired for double duty, combining their interests in biochemistry and animal physiology.

One additional pilot investigation carried out for this paper was an analysis of the journals most frequently referred to in six widely used biochemistry texts. As a historical comparison to test the stability of the current list, a matching set of six texts from the period 1968–1971 was constructed and similarly analyzed (see Appendix 3 for the list of tests). Table 4 presents, for those serials scoring at least one percent of the total in any text, the rankings arranged by number of texts in which the one percent measure was exceeded. In the table, those serials primarily devoted to review articles or regularly publishing review articles are indicated.

Table 3. Publication Habits of Biochemists in Liberal Arts Colleges

1972-78   (39 schools)   1965-71   (23 schools)
          Articles (Number) in Indicated Journals

1. Comparative Biochemistry Physiology (19)
2. Biochem. Biophys. Res. Commun. (18)
3. Nature (10)
4. Biochemistry (7)
5. Science (7)
6. Arch. Biochem. Biophys. (6)
7. Biochim. Biophys. Acta (6)
8. J. Am. Chem. Soc. (5)
9. Analyt. Biochem. (4)
10. Biopolymers (4)
11. J. Biol. Chem. (4)
12. Bioorganic Chem. (3)
13. FEBS Letters (3)
14. J. Histochem. Cytochem. (3)
15. J. Nat. Cancer Inst. (3)
16. Mutation Res. (3)
17. Proc. Nat. Acad. Sci. (3)
18. Steroids (3)
19. Canad. J. Biochem. (2)
20. Immunol. (2)
21. J. Lipid Res. (2)
22. J. Membrane Biochem. (2)
23. J. Mol. Biol. (2)
24. Thrombosis Haemostasis (2)
    All Others (22)

Biochem. Biophys. Res. Commun. (15)
J. Am. Chem. Soc. (15)
Biochim. Biophys. Acta (11)
Comp. Biochem. Physiol. (11)
Biochemistry (11)
Nature (11)
Proc. Nat. Acad. Sci. (6)
Arch. Biochem. Biophys. (5)
J. Biol. Chem. (4)
Science (4)
Analyt. Biochem. (3)
Canad. J. Biochem. (3)
J. Mol. Biol. (3)
Biochem. J. (2)
J. Chromat. (2)
All Others (17)

Abstracts (Number) in Indicated Journals

1. Fed. Proc. (12)
2. Biophys. J. (6)
3. Proc. Soc. Exp. Med. Biol. (1)

Fed. Proc. (8)
Biophys. J. (3)
J. Dent. Res. (1)

The following observations may be noted:

1. Many of the journals favored for authorship by American biochemists appear.

2. There is a strong dominance of review serials and other journals that regularly carry review articles.

It is apparent that a library that serves organized instructional needs should seriously consider including some of these latter titles, particu-

Table 4. Journals Cited in Six Widely Used Biochemistry Texts with Average Citation Share in Those Texts.

1980 Texts

Journals Cited in Six Texts with Percentage of Citations

1. Annu. Rev. Biochem.*   14.3
2. Science*   9.2
3. Sci. Am.   8.2
4. Nature*   7.5
5. Advan. Enzymol.*   3.7
6. Curr. Top. Cell Regul.*   1.8

Journals Cited in Five Texts with Percentage of Citations

1. Proc. Nat. Acad. Sci.   7.6
2. J. Biol. Chem.   6.8
3. New Eng. J. Med.   4.3
4. J. Mol. Biol.   4.0

Journals Cited in Four Texts with Percentage of Citations

1. Fed. Proc.*   2.5
2. Cold Spring Harb. Symp. Quant. Biol.   2.3
3. Biochemistry   2.3
4. Biochim.Biophys.Acta   2.3
5. Adv. Protein Chem.*   2.3

Journals Cited in Three Texts with Percentage of Citations

1. Essays in Biochem.*   3.7
2. Arch. Biochem. Biophys.   1.7
3. Biochem. J.   1.7

Journals Cited in Two Texts with Percentage of Citations

1. Annu. Rev. Physiol.*   3.0
2. Physiol. Revs.*   3.0
3. FEBS Letters   2.0
4. Meth. Enzymol.*   2.0
5. Vitamins and Hormones*   2.0
6. Eur. J. Biochem.   1.5
7. Ann. NY Acad. Sci.*   1.0
8. Bacteriol. Rev.*   1.0
9. Horizons in Biochem. and Biophys.*   1.0
10. Prog. Biophys. Mol. Biol.* 1.0

1968-71 Texts

Journals Cited in Six Texts with Percentage of Citations

1. Annu. Rev. Biochem.*   16.8
2. Science*   8.4
3. Nature*   5.6
4. Advan. Enzymol.*   3.4
5. Fed. Proc.*   1.3

Journals Cited in Five Texts with Percentage of Citations

1. J. Biol. Chem.   15.0
2. J. Mol. Biol.   4.5
3. Biochem. J.   2.6

Journals Cited in Four Texts with Percentage of Citations

1. Proc. Nat. Acad. Sci.   11.7
2. Biochemistry   4.7

Journals Cited in Three Texts with Percentage of Citations

1. Angew.Chem.Int.Ed.Eng.*   4.5
2. Sci. Am.*   4.0
3. J. Am. Chem. Soc.   3.4
4. Biochem. Biophys. Res.Comm. 2.7
5. Harvey Lect.*   1.8
6. Prog.Nucl.Acid.Res.Molec. Biol.*   1.7
7. Adv. Protein Chem.*   1.5

Journals Cited in Two Texts with Percentage of Citations

1. Annu. Rev. Plant Physiol.* 5.2
2. Biochim.Biophys. Acta   3.5
3. Proc.Roy.Soc.Lond.B   2.2
4. Arch. Biochem. Biophys.   2.0
5. Vitamins and Hormones*   1.7
6. Eur. J. Biochem.   1.6
7. J. Clin. Invest.   1.6
8. Advan. Carb. Chem.*   1.5
9. Advan. Enzyme Regul.*   1.2

*Journals that regularly feature review-type articles.

larly in light of their strength over time (as noted in the historical group). The Garfield study particularly mentions the importance of review serials.

The Final Selection Decision

Although journal lists based on any school of selection are helpful, the librarian is the final decision-maker, often faced with a selection decision on a journal recommended by an important patron. Some helpful suggestions follow for that ultimate decision on an unknown journal.

1. Has the patron seen or used the journal? If not, *Current Contents* entry pages from past issues should be given to him to examine for appropriateness of language of publication and subject.

2. Use the Author and Address Index of *Current Contents* for as many issues as possible to determine authorship orientation. Is your type and level of institution regularly represented? Does this journal show promise for authors of your type of institution?

3. Consult as many Citing Journal Packages as possible from *Science Citation Index Annuals*. What journal does this candidate journal habitually cite year after year? Does the subject orientation derived from this agree with the patron's conceptions of what the journal is about?

4. Consult as many Cited Journal Packages as possible from the *Science Citation Index Annuals*. What use is made of the articles from this journal? Have better known journals in this field cited this candidate journal often?

5. How does this journal compare in gross citations or citations per article published with comparable journals?

6. Calculate the cost of subscribing to the journal versus legitimate Interlibrary Loan fees when the Copyright Clearance Charge is also regularly paid. (A sample issue will contain, at the bottom of the first page of each article, the fee for copying.) consider the use of legitimate commercial article suppliers such as the Institute of Scientific Information's *OATS* service. It may well be worth suggesting to your patron that you might provide him with either of these forms of services rather than subscribing to the journal.

The point in making these suggestions is not to avoid purchase, but merely to note that librarians have much more information at their command than they suppose and that they should use all that information before committing several hundred dollars per year for years to come for a journal of unknown value.

The Older Stock

The final issues to be addressed here are the interlocking questions of back-year purchases and older-volume retirement. Research by both indirect (Smith, 1970; Tibbetts, 1974) and direct (Schlomann & Ahl, 1979) methods yields a 15–20 year active-life estimate for most journals. This may also be accepted as the outside limit for retrospective holdings. For journals involving foreign languages, particularly German, recent work indicates that the trend towards anglicization is at most 15 years old and closer to 10 in some cases (Stankus, Schlessinger, & Schlessinger, 1981). Finally, a new citation ranking table in *JCR*, the "Half-Life" table, shows that the bulk of references to biochemical journals are to papers at most 10 years old.

REFERENCES

Cass, James, & Birnbaum, Max. *Comparative Guide to American Colleges*. New York: Harper and Row, 1978.

Cattell Press. *Industrial Research Laboratories of the U.S*. New York: R.R. Bowker, 1970.

Chen, Ching-Chih. *Scientific and Technical Information Sources*. Cambridge, MA: MIT Press, 1975.

Garfield, Eugene. Citation Analysis as a Tool in Journal Evaluation. *Science*, 1972, *178*, 471–9.

Garfield, Eugene. *Essays of an Information Scientist*. Philadelphia: ISI Press, 1977.

Garfield, Eugene. *SCI Journal Citation Reports*. Philadelphia: ISI Press, 1975.

Garfield Eugene. Trends in Biochemical Literature. *Trends in Biochemical Sciences*, 1979, *4*, 290–5.

Katz, Bill, and Richard Berry. *Magazines for Libraries*. New York: R.R. Bowker, 1978.

Malinowski, H. Robert, Gray, Richard, & Gary, Dorothy. *Science and Engineering Literature*. Littleton, Co: Libraries Unlimited, 1976.

Mount, Ellis. *University Science and Engineering Libraries*. Westport, CT: Greenwood Press, 1975.

Schloman, Barbara, and Ahl, Ruth. Retention Periods for Journals in a Small Academic Library. *Special Libraries*, 1979, *70*, 377–83.

Sengupta, I.N. Recent Growth of the Literature of Biochemistry and Changes in Ranking of Periodicals. *Journal of Documentation*, 1973, *29*, 192–211.

Smith, Joan. A Periodical Use Study at Children's Hospital of Michigan. *Bulletin of the Medical Library Association*. 1970, *58*, 65–7.

Stankus, Tony, Schlessinger, Rashelle, & Schlessinger, Bernard S. English-Language Article Publication in German Basic Science Journals. *Science and Technology Libraries*, 1981, in press.

Stankus, Tony, and Rice, Barbara. Handle with Care: Use and Citation Data for Science Journal Management. *Collection Development*, 1981, in press.

Strauss, Lucille, Sheve, Irene, & Brown, Alberta. *Scientific and Technical Libraries*. New York: Becker and Hayes, 1972.

Tibbets, Pamela. A Method for Estimating the In-House Use of the Periodical Collection in the University of Minnesota Biomedical Library. *Bulletin of the Medical Library Association*, 1974, *64*, 37–48.

Appendix 1. Journals Noted Within the Paper
             Collection Development: Journals for Biochemists

1. Acta Biochimica et Biophysica (G)
2. Acta Biochimica Polonica (G)
3. Advances in Enzymology and Related Areas of Molecular
    Biology (G)
4. Advances in Protein Chemistry
5. Agricultural and Biological Chemistry - Tokyo (G)
6. American Journal of Physiology (G)
7. Analytical Biochemistry (G)
8. Analytical Chemistry (G)
9. Annals of the New York Academy of Sciences (G)
10. Annual Review of Biochemistry (G)
11. Annual Review of Physiology
12. Archives of Biochemistry and Biophysics (G)
13. Bacteriological Reviews (G)
14. Biochemical and Biophysical Research Communications (G)
15. Biochemical Genetics
16. Biochemical Journal (G)
17. Biochemical Pharmacology (G)
18. Biochemical Society Transactions (G)
19. Biochemistry - U.S. (G)
20. Biochimica et Biophysica Acta (G)
21. Biochimie (G)
22. Bioinorganic Chemistry (G)
23. Biokhimiya (Biochemistry - USSR)
24. Biology of Reproduction
25. Bioorganic Chemistry (G)
26. Bioorganicheskaya Khimiya (G)
27. Biophysical Journal
28. Biopolymers (G)
29. Canadian Journal of Biochemistry (G)
30. Cancer Research (G)
31. Carbohydrate Research
32. Cell (G)
33. Cereal Chemistry
34. Chemistry and Physics of Lipids (G)
35. Clinica Chimica Acta
36. Clinical Biochemistry
37. Clinical Chemistry
38. Clinical Research
39. Cold Spring Harbor Symposia (G)
40. Comparative Biochemistry
41. CRC Critical REviews in Biochemistry (G)
42. Current Topics in Cellular Regulation
43. Cytogenetics Cell Genetics
44. Endocrinology (G)
45. Enzymes (G)
46. Essays in Biochemistry
47. European Journal of Biochemistry (G)

Appendix 1 (Cont.)

48. Experientia
49. Experimental Cell Research (G)
50. FEBS Letters (G)
51. Federation Proceedings (G)
52. Food and Cosmetic Toxicology
53. Gene
54. Hoppe-Seyler's Zeitschrift Fuer Physiologische Chemie (G)
55. Horizons in Biochemistry and Biophysics
56. Immunology
57. Indian Journal of Biochemistry and Biophysics (G)
58. International Journal of Biochemistry (G)
59. International Journal of Peptide and Protein Research (G)
60. Italian Journal of Biochemistry (G)
61. Journal of Agricultural and Food Chemistry
62. Journal of Bacteriology (G)
63. Journal of Biochemistry-Tokyo (G)
64. Journal of Biological Chemistry (G)
65. Journal of Cell Biology (G)
66. Journal of Cellular Physiology
67. Journal of Chromatography (G)
68. Journal of Clinical Investigation (G)
69. Journal of Cyclic Nucleotide Research (G)
70. Journal of Dental Research
71. Journal of Experimental Medicine (G)
72. Journal of Food Science
73. Journal of General Microbiology (G)
74. Journal of General Physiology (G)
75. Journal of General Virology
76. Journal of Histochemistry and Cytochemistry
77. Journal of Immunology
78. Journal of Laboratory and Clinical Medicine
79. Journal of Lipid Research (G)
80. Journal of Membrane Biochemistry
81. Journal of Molecular Biology (G)
82. Journal of Molecular Evolution
83. Journal of Neurochemistry (G)
84. Journal of Nutrition (G)
85. Journal of Physiology - London (G)
86. Journal of Supramolecular Structure
87. Journal of the American Chemical Society (G)
88. Journal of the American Oil Chemists Society
89. Journal of the Association of Official Analytical Chemists (G)
90. Journal of the National Cancer Institute
91. Journal of Virology (G)
92. Life Sciences (G)
93. Lipids (G)
94. Methods of Enzymology (G)
95. Molecular and Cellular Biochemistry (G)
96. Molecular and General Genetics (G)

Appendix 1 (Cont.)

97. Molecular Pharmacology (G)
98. Mutation Research
99. Nature (G)
100. Naturwissenschaften
101. New England Journal of Medicine
102. Nucleic Acids Research (G)
103. Pediatric Research
104. Physiological Chemistry and Physics (G)
105. Physiological Reviews
106. Physiologist
107. Phytochemistry (G)
108. Plant Physiology (G)
109. Postepy Biochemii (G)
110. Preparative Biochemistry (G)
111. Proceedings of the American Association For Cancer Research (a special issue of Cancer Research)
112. Proceedings of the National Academy of Sciences - USA (G)
113. Proceedings of the Societies for Experimental Biology and Medicine (G)
114. Progress in Biophysics and Molecular Biology
115. Revue Romaine de Biochimie (G)
116. Science (G)
117. Seikagaku (G)
118. Steroids
119. Thrombosis Haemostasis
120. Toxicology and Applied Pharmacology
121. Ukrainskii Biokhimicheskii Zhurnal (G)
122. Virology (G)
123. Vitamins and Hormones

(G) - included on Garfield's lists.

Appendix 2. Selected Units Studied in Table 1.

Selection of the units in this appendix was made from the indicated sources with attention paid to geographical diversity, type of institution, and specific biochemical orientation.

Medical Schools

Selection Source: Garfield, Eugene. "Most-Cited Articles of the 1960's 3. Preclinical Basic Research."
Current Contents, 1980, <u>23</u>, 5-13.

    East: Harvard University
                  School of Medicine, Boston, MA
                  (Dept. Biol. Chem.)

                  Cornell University
                  College of Medicine, New York City, NY
                  (Dept. Biochem.)

                  New York University
                  Medical Center, New York City, NY
                  (Dept. Biochem.)

  Midwest: Case-Western Reserve University
                  School of Medicine, Cleveland, OH
                  (Dept. Biochem.)

                  University of Chicago
                  Pritzker School of Medicine, Chicago, IL
                  (Dept. Biochem.)

                  Washington University of St. Louis
                  School of Medicine, St. Louis, MO
                  (Dept. Biochem.)

    South: Vanderbilt University
                  School of Medicine, Nashville, TN
                  (Dept. Biochem.)

                  Duke University
                  Medical Center, Durham, NC
                  (Dept. Biochem.)

App. 2.

    West: University of Washington at Seattle
School of Medicine, Seattle, WA
(Dept. Biochem.)

          University of California at San Francisco
Medical School, San Francisco, CA
(Dept. Biochem.)

Universities

Selection Source: Roose, Kenneth, and Anderson, Charles. A Rating of Graduate School Programs. Washington, DC American Council on Education, 1970.

    East: Princeton University
Princeton, NJ
(Dept. Biochem.)

          Brandeis University
Waltham, MA
(Dept. and Graduate Dept. Biochem.)

          M.I.T.
Cambridge, MA
(Depts. Biol. and Chem.)

    Midwest: University of Illinois
Urbana-Champaign, IL
(Dept. Biochem.)

          Purdue University
West Lafayette, IN
(Dept. Biochem.)

          Indiana University
Bloomington, IN
(Dept. Biol. Sciences and Chem.)

    South: Oklahoma State University
Stillwater, OK
(Dept. Biochem.)

App. 2.

           Florida State University
           Tallahassee, FL
           (Depts. Biol.; Chem.; Inst. Mol. Biophys.)

West: Caltech
       Pasadena, CA
       (Depts. Biol.; Chem.)

       University of Oregon
       Eugene, OR
       (Inst. Molec. Biol.)

Independent, Non-Profit Research Foundations

   Selection Source: Association of Independent Research Institutes. Constitution and Bylaws. 1977.

      East: The Wistar Institute
             Philadelphia, PA
             (All article output examined.)

             The Worcester Foundation For Experimental Biology
             Shrewsbury, MA
             (All article output examined.)

Midwest: Cancer Research Center
             Columbia, MO
             (All article output examined.)

             Michigan Cancer Foundation
             Detroit, MI
             (All article output examined.)

             Mayo Clinic and Research Foundation
             Rochester, MN
             (Depts. Biochem. and Molec. Medicine)
             Note: Mayo Clinic is not a member of this
             Association and does have medical school ties, but
             national reputation and need for geographic representation
             helped its inclusion.

     South: Oklahoma Medical Research Foundation and Inst.
             Oklahoma City, OK
             (All article output checked.)

             Papanicolau Cancer Research Inst.
             Miami, FL
             (All article output checked.)

      West: Salk Inst. Biological Studies
             San Diego, CA
             (All article output checked.)

App. 2.

                Pasadena Found. for Medical Research
                Pasadena, CA
                (All article output checked.)

                Scripps Clinic and Research Foundation
                La Jolla, CA
                (Dept. Biochem.)

Federal, Veterans and Military

      Selection Source: Author's study of available institutes in
                            Washington, DC and other areas.

         East: Veterans Administration Hospital
                Buffalo, NY
                (All article output checked.)

                U.S. Food and Drug Administration
                Bethesda, MD
                (Bureau of Biologics examined.)

                National Cancer Institute
                Bethesda, MD
                (Biochem. Lab.)

                National Inst. of Arthritis, Metabolic
                Diseases and Diabetes
                Bethesda, MD
                (Molec. Biol. Lab.)

                National Inst. Dental Research
                Bethesda, MD
                (Biochem. Lab.)

                Walter Reed Army Inst.
                Washington, DC
                (Dept. Biochem.)

     Midwest: Veterans Administration Hospital
                Ann Arbor, MI
                (All article output checked.)

       South: Veterans Administration Hospital
                New Orleans, LA
                (All article output examined.)

                Center for Disease Control
                Atlanta, GA
                (All article output examined.)

        West: Veterans Administration Hospital
                Palo Alto, CA
                (All article output checked.)

Appendix 3. Texts Used for Data in Table 4.

Current Group

    Bohinski, Robert C., Modern Concepts in Biochemistry. 3rd edition, Boston: Allyn and Bacon, 1979.

    Lehninger, Albert L. Biochemistry: The Molecular Basis of All Structure and Function. New York: Worth, 1975.

    McGilvery, Robert W. Biochemistry: A Functional Approach. Philadelphia: Saunders, 1979.

    Metzler, David E. Biochemistry: The Chemical Reactions of Living Cells. New York: Academic Press, 1977.

    Stryer, Lubert. Biochemistry. San Francisco: W. H. Freeman, 1975.

    White, Abraham, et al. Principles of Biochemistry. 6th edition, New York: McGraw-Hill, 1978.

Historical Comparison Group

    Harrow, Benjamin and Mazur, Abraham. Textbook of Bio-Chemistry. 10th edition. Philadelphia: Saunders, 1971.

    Lehninger, Albert L. Biochemistry. New York: Worth, 1970

    Mahler, Henry R. and Cordes, Eugene H. Biological Chemistry. New York: Harper and Row, 1968.

    Mallette, M. Frank, et al. Introductory Biochemistry. Baltimore: Williams and Wilkins, 1971.

    McGilvery, Robert W. Biochemistry: A Functional Approach. Philadelphia: Saunders, 1970.

    White, Abraham, et al. Principles of Biochemistry. New York: McGraw-Hill, 1968.

BIBLIOGRAPHIC CONTROL: INDEXING AND ABSTRACTING SERVICES IN BIOCHEMISTRY—A CHRONOLOGICAL AND HISTORICAL APPROACH

Judith A. Douville

ABSTRACT. An overview of the indexing and abstracting services important to biochemistry is presented, preceded by an introductory history of this type of literature. Content and format of the major services are described, together with their bibliographic history. A review of on-line bibliographic services is also included as a modern complement to the older, traditional forms of bibliographic control.

Early Services

The earliest services which could be said to include material now classified as "biochemical" were probably the medical services. Collison (1971) reports numerous services, beginning as early as 1830. Chemical and pharmaceutical journals, which often carried like material, also began to be published about this time. A list of these follows.

Pharmaceutisches Central-Blatt (Berlin Academy, Leipzig and Berlin), 1830–1849//.

American Medical Intelligencer: A Concentrated Record of Medical Science and Literature (Philadelphia), 1837–1842// superseded by:

Medical News and Library, 1843–1879//.

Half-Yearly Abstract of the Medical Sciences: Being a Digest of British and Continental Medicine and of the Progress of Medi-

---

Judith A. Douville is Technical Librarian, TRC Environmental Consultants, Inc., 125 Silas Deane Highway, Wethersfield, CT 06109.

cine and the Collateral Sciences, (London, by W.H. Ranking), 1845–1873//; (Philadelphia, American Edition), 1845–1873//.

Chemisch-Pharmaceutisches Central-Blatt, 1850–1855//; supersedes Pharmaceutisches Central-Blatt. Superseded by:

Chemisches Central-Blatt, 1856–1906//.

Monthly Abstract of Medical Science, 1874–1879//; supersedes Half-Yearly Abstract . . .

Medical News and Abstract, 1880–1881//; supersedes Medical News and Library, and in turn was superseded by:

Medical News, 1882–1905//.

Annales de Chimie Analytique, Appliquee a l'Industrie, a l'Agriculture, a la Pharmacie, et a la Biologie (Centre de Documentaton Chimique, Paris), 1896–1918//.

International Record of Medicine (New York), 1882–1905//; supersedes Medical News.

These early attempts to bring a distillation of the literature to researchers and practitioners were, in many cases, short-lived; some were not well-financed and others suffered the loss of editors or patrons. It does not seem possible that loss of readership could be blamed.

As time went on, the numbers of new services diminished, because the services themselves became more established, as can be seen from the list that follows.

Chemical Abstracts, 1907 to present, about which more will be said later.

Biochemisches Zentralblatt (Germany), 1902–1909//, which became:

Zentralblatt fur Biochemie und Biophysik (Germany), 1909–1918//, which was superseded by:

Berichte uber die gesamte Physiologie und experimentelle Pharmakologie, 1918 to present. This title forms Abteilung A, formerly titled Berichte uber die wissenschaftliche Biologie: Biochemistry—Biology (Crane, 1957, p.143). There are 18 volumes annually; Springer Verlag is the publisher.

Chemisches Zentralblatt: vollstandiges Repertorium fur all Zweige der reinen und angewandten Chemie, 1907–1969//; this title superseded *Chemisches Central-Blatt*.

Referativnyi Meditsinskii Zhurnal (Moscow), 1920–1923//.

British Abstracts, 1926–1953//, which continued the abstracts sections found in *Journal of the Chemical Society*, 1871–1925, and *Journal of the Society of Chemical Industry*, 1882–1925.

Further discussion of medically oriented titles is beyond the scope of this paper.

Major Services Since 1925

As of 1925, there did not seem to be any abstracting or indexing service devoted completely to biochemistry, although *Chemical Abstracts*, mentioned above, is now considered to be one of the world's foremost abstracting and indexing services for biochemistry.

At this time, the American Association for the Advancement of Science, the Union of American Biological Societies, and the National Academy of Sciences united to found the service *Biological Abstracts*, from the union of *Botanical Abstracts* (1918–1925//) and *Abstracts of Bacteriology* (1917–1925//).

Biological Abstracts

Biological Abstracts, begun in 1926, is a semi-monthly abstracting service of international scope, with very comprehensive coverage of the field. In 1974, there were 623 subject categories of abstracts. Abstracts are in English, with abstract titles in English and the original language of the article. All authors are named, and the senior author's affiliation is given.

Four indexes are provided:

1. Author, personal and corporate.
2. Biosystematic (since July 1963), listing references according to taxonomy.
3. CROSS (Computer Rearrangement of Subject Specialties), which enables searchers to find subjects covered in articles other than those of major subject emphasis.

4. Subject (BASIC) (Malinowsky, 1976, p.160), (Biological Abstracts Subjects in Context), 1962 to present, consisting of author's chosen title plus significant terms selected from the article to augment or clarify the title.

This last service is computer produced to reduce the time-lag in the production of subject indexes, which were two years behind at the time of its inception. Additionally, *Bioresearch Index* (Owen, 1974, p.7) has been published monthly since 1965 (Chen, 1977) as an auxiliary index to provide access to research papers in addition to those found in *Biological Abstracts*, to complete the coverage of the biological sciences. Unfortunately, no cumulative indexes to *Bioresearch Index* were ever produced, nor do any seem to be forthcoming. *Bioresearch Index* was entitled *BioResearch Titles* from its inception in 1965 until 1967.

Biological Abstracts is now published by BioSciences Information Service (BIOSIS) in Philadelphia.

Chemical Abstracts

According to Bottle (1971), the biochemical content of *Chemical Abstracts* in 1971 was about 28%, corresponding to approximately 70,000 abstracts annually of interest to biologists. This number of abstracts is nearly half the number appearing in *Biological Abstracts* and indicates the status of *Chemical Abstracts* as a service of major importance to biochemists. It would be expected that the coverage has not changed appreciably since 1971.

Chemical Abstracts has been published continuously since 1907 and, at the present, is the world's largest and most comprehensive indexing and abstracting service. Before 1935, the coverage was less comprehensive, and searchers of that previous period would be well-advised to check *Chemisches Zentralblatt* and *British Abstracts*, and also their precursors, to ensure complete coverage.

Chemical Abstracts now publishes separate section groupings. One of these, Biochemical Sections, the most important to biochemists, is available at a lower cost than the entire subscription to the full *Chemical Abstracts*. However, one must still use the full indexes for thorough searching of the biochemical sections, since only keyword indexes are provided in the separate section groupings.

General indexes are available for all of *Chemical Abstracts:* author, patent number and concordance, formula, ring systems, and subject (now subdivided into Chemical Substance index and General Subject index). Cumulative indexes are also available, covering ten year periods up to 1956, and five year periods since that date. A more detailed description of *Chemical Abstracts* is beyond the scope of this paper.

Bulletin Signaletique

Originally named *Bulletin Analytique,* and renamed in 1956, this service has been produced since 1940 by the Centre National de la Recherche Scientifique, part of the Ministry of Education in Paris (Bottle, 1967). This service offers indicative abstracts in numerous sections in the sciences. Since volume 12, 1961, *Section 12, Biophysique, Biochimie, Chimie Analytique* (Owen, 1974) (now *Section 320, Biochimie, Biophysique)* (NFSAIS, 1963), of interest to biochemists, has existed. Issues appear monthly, with author indexes. Full bibliographic information is given; the brief abstracts are in French. The classification scheme in the entire service has been recently revised and expanded, according to the PASCAL system, and sections have been renumbered.

Excerpta Medica

First published by the Dutch organization Excerpta Medica Foundation in 1947, *Excerpta Medica* covered important literature back to 1939 (Bottle, 1971). Monthly issues, printed in English, are currently published in 39 sections, all available separately. Monthly and annual author indexes are available, and there is an annual subject index. Both author and subject indexes are computer produced. Of interest to biochemists is *Section 2, Physiology, Biochemistry, Pharmacology, and Toxicology,* begun in 1948. A newer section, *Section 29: Biochemistry* (vol. 18, 1965 to present), now more closely covers the biochemical field (Malinowsky, 1976). The consecutively numbered and informative abstracts are classified into divisions and subdivisions. Timeliness has recently been improved, with computerization undoubtedly aiding in this task.

Following the appearance of *Excerpta Medica* in 1947, several other abstracting services of some importance to biochemistry were introduced. *Abstracts of Vitamin Literature, 1947–1949//* was replaced by *Vitamin Abstracts* in 1949, both produced by the Association of Vitamin Chemists. In 1953, *Abstracts of Bioanalytic Technology, 1953–1965//* was issued by the American Association of Bioanalysts, Chicago. In 1947, *International Medical Abstracts and Reviews* was begun, and was continued in 1956 by *Journal of Medicine and International Medical Abstracts and Reviews* (Collison, 1971).

Referativnyi Zhurnal-Biologiia

In 1953, the Akademiia Nauk, SSSR, Institut Nauchnoi Informatsii (VINITII) issued the first of a vast series of separate abstracting journals, the *Referativnyi Zhurnal*. Abstracts are in Russian (Bottle, 1971).

The semi-monthly issues are comparable in size with *Biological Abstracts* and are most useful for learning about newly available material in Soviet bloc journals, before that material becomes available in other abstracting services. There are annual author and subject indexes.

The *Biologiia* section became an offshoot, in 1954, of the *Khimiia* section. In 1955, the biological chemistry abstracts became available as *Referativnyi Zhurnal: Khimiia (Biologicheskaia Khimiia)* (Owen, 1974; NFSAIS, 1963). There is no separate subject index; the index for the *Khimiia* must be used.

British Abstracts

In 1953, *British Abstracts,* which had gone through numerous regroupings and section changes since its inception in 1926, ceased publication due to lack of funds. Several sections survived with new names, one of which was Series A, Section 3, which at first became *British Abstracts of Medical Science,* 1954–1956 (Malinowsky, 1976), and then was changed to *International Abstracts of Biological Sciences,* 1956 to present (Bottle, 1971; NFSAIS, 1963). Now published by Pergamon Press, it scans over 500 major journals and produces over 35,000 abstracts annually. Volume indexes (author, subject, and taxonomic) are published annually. The journal is available as separate sections: *Physiology* and *Biochemistry/Biophysics*.

Other offshoots of *British Abstracts* include *Journal of the Science of Food and Agriculture,* the *Appendix* of which is of interest to biochemists, and *Analytical Abstracts,* mentioned later.

Other Useful Services

There are several other lesser-known abstracting services from other parts of the world which are of importance to biochemists. One of these is *Tampakushitsu, Kakusan, Koso* (Protein-Nucleic Acids-Enzymes), Section on *Abstracts of Foreign Literature*, published by the Koryitsu Shuppan Company, Ltd., Tokyo. First issued in 1956, it is published monthly (NFSAIS, 1963). Another is *Abstracts of Bulgarian Scientific Literature: Biology and Medicine*, which began in 1958 and later diversified and became *Abstracts of Bulgarian Scientific Literature*, sections on *Medicine and Physical Culture* (in 1958) and *Biology and Biochemistry* (in 1962) (Collison, 1971), the latter a quarterly covering about 35 Bulgarian journals annually (NFSAIS, 1963; FID, 1969). Still another is a quarterly entitled *Studii si Cercetari de Biochimie: Section Recenzii*, issued in 1958 by the Academia Republicii Populare Romine, Institutul de Biochimie, Bucharest, Rumania (NFSAIS, 1963).

There are several older services of interest to biochemists, which are not devoted to the subject field exclusively but do contain items which should be noted by researchers. One of these is *Biological and Agricultural Index*, first begun in 1916 as *Agricultural Index* by the H.W. Wilson Company and bearing its present title since 1964. It is a subject-alphabetized indexing service and does not contain abstracts (Malinowsky, 1976). Another is *Dissertation Abstracts* (1938–1965) and since volume 27, 1966, its *Section B: The Sciences and Engineering*, which contains new research presented in doctoral dissertations.

Since the early 1960s, several newer services have appeared which provide more abstracting and indexing access for biochemical researchers. These include:

1. *Science Citation Index*, not a conventional abstracting service such as those discussed before. First published in 1963 as a quarterly, by the Institute for Scientific Information in Philadelphia, this service notes what articles, books, etc. are being cited in currently published articles. A study of the patterns of citation activity can lead to information concerning important areas of activity in the sciences. There are annual and five-year index cumulations for this service.

2. *Pandex Current Index to Scientific and Technical Literature*, an interdisciplinary indexing service, retrospectively issued in microform covering 1967–1968, and currently published by CCM Information Corporation in New York, beginning with volume 1 in 1969 (Koltay, 1977). It indexes about 2400 journals, 6000 books, 5000 selected patents, and 35,000 U.S. technical reports (Bottle, 1971).

3. *Abstracts of Communications* (Collison, 1971), published by the Federation of European Biochemical Societies (FEBS) in 1964 (it is not known if this service has continued).

4. *Clinical Biochemistry*, published by Kogan Page, beginning in 1969, with selective coverage of the literature by abstracts grouped under ten headings, with each group preceded by a review of recent research.

5. *East European Scientific Abstracts: Biomedical Sciences*, published since 1964 by the Joint Publications Research Service (part of the U.S. Department of Commerce) under the auspices of the National Technical Information Service on a monthly or biweekly basis. What appears to be a companion series, *U.S.S.R. Scientific Abstracts-Biomedical Abstracts*, was started in 1964 and issued weekly.

6. *Novinky Literatury-Prirodni Vedy, Rada Khemicka*, issued since 1964 in ten numbers annually, 150 abstracts per year, by Statni Knohovna CSSR, Prague, Czechoslovakia. Time lag is about 9–12 months.

7. *Resumenes de Articulos Cientificos y Technicos-Serie A. Quimica Industrial (Subseries 2: Bioquimica, Productos Farmaceuticos*, begun in 1962, and published by Centro de Informacion y Documentacion, Madrid, Spain. Time lag is about four months, and annual coverage of *Serie A* is about 18,000 abstracts. Approximately 100 Spanish and 1500 foreign journals are covered. Author indexes are published annually (FID, 1969).

8. In addition one should note *Federation Proceedings, Nutrition Abstracts and Reviews* (since 1931), and *Analytical Abstracts* (Society for Analytical Chemistry), the last formed from Part C, *British Abstracts*, all important to biochemistry, although their treatment of the field is narrow (Bottle, 1971).

Recent Services

Several newer services important to biochemistry deserve mention here. Published since 1970, they depend upon the newer techniques of computer-aided production, in order to reduce the time lag from journal article to the reader.

1. *Nucleic Acids Abstracts*, a monthly published by Information Retrieval Ltd., London, began in 1971. *Amino Acids, Peptide and Protein Abstracts*, begun in 1972, is a companion publication.

2. *Biogenic Amines and Transmitters in the Nervous System*, 1970 to present, is a semi-monthly publication from the Brain Information Service, Brain Research Institute, UCLA, and is cosponsored by the

National Institute of Neurological and Communicative Disease and Stroke, U.S. HEW.

3. *Current Contents: Agriculture, Biology, and Environmental Sciences,* 1970 to present, a product of the Institute for Scientific Information, Philadelphia, is not an abstracting service, but a current-awareness service which reproduces the title pages of select journals. Articles desired can be obtained from ISI.

4. *Chemical-Biological Activities* (Koltay, 1977), published by the Chemical Abstracts Service, was a biweekly abstracting service devoted to the biological activities of organic compounds. First published in 1965, it ceased with volume 13 in 1971. It had author, molecular formula, KWIC (keyword-in-context), and semi-annual cumulated indexes (Sheehy, 1976).

Computer-Readable Data Bases

Beginning with the early 1970s, many of the manually used data bases discussed previously in this paper became available in computer-readable form and are now accessed through commercial vendors (Capitol Systems Group, 1978).

Biological Abstracts (with *Bioresearch Index*) is available from Lockheed Information Systems, Palo Alto, California and Systems Development Corporation (SDC), Santa Monica, California, beginning with 1969; and from Bibliographic Retrieval Services (BRS), Scotia, New York, from 1970 on. Lockheed's version is named BIOSIS Previews 69–71 (file 55) and BIOSIS Previews (file 5) for the most recent material, 1972 to date. SDC's version is BIOSIS/BIO6973; a separate companion file, named BIOCODES, unique to SDC, enables the user to access taxonomic information and cross references. BRS' coverage of *Biological Abstracts* is similar to Lockheed's.

Chemical Abstracts' biochemically oriented material is also available on-line: Lockheed supplies CA SEARCH files 2, 3, 4 (file 2 covers 1967–71, file 3, 1972–1976, and file 4, 1977 to date). Lockheed also provides two more companion files: CHEMSEARCH (file 30), a directory of the most recently cited chemical substances in file 4, with the capability of providing access to very new substances via Chemical Abstracts Registry Numbers; and CHEMNAME (file 31), a dictionary-type listing of chemical substances for searching convenience. Items selected for inclusion in file 31 must have been referenced two or more times in the 9th Collective Chemical Abstracts Index Period.

SDC similarly supplies *Chemical Abstracts* via CHEM 7071 (for 1970–1971), CAS 7276 (for 1972–1976), and CAS 77. for 1977 to date. A companion file, CHEMDEX, is similar to Lockheed's CHEMNAME. BRS has coverage of *Chemical Abstracts* beginning with 1970.

CHEMLINE, produced through joint effort by the National Library of Medicine (NLM) and Chemical Abstracts Service, is an on-line listing of names of chemical substances (similar to Lockheed's CHEMNAME), and is available through the MEDLARS network from NLM and State University of New York at Albany. In 1978, there were about 250,000 items in the file.

Excerpta Medica, from June 1974 on, is available through Lockheed as files 72 and 73 and corresponds directly with the printed version.

National Technical Information Service (NTIS) material is available from BRS and SDC (as file NTIS) from 1970 to the present; from Lockheed, NTIS is available from 1964 on (file 6). NTIS covers all U.S. government-sponsored technical research reports including those of biochemical interest; the data base corresponds to the printed selective *Weekly Government Abstracts* newsletters and the all-inclusive *Government Reports Announcements.*

Nutrition Abstracts and Reviews, mentioned previously, is available on-line as part of Lockheed's CAB ABSTRACTS (file 50), produced by the Commonwealth Agricultural Bureaux, and covers 1973 to the present.

SCISEARCH, file 34 from Lockheed, is the computer-readable version of *Science Citation Index (SCI).* Available coverage extends from 1974 to the present. Additional items covered by *Current Contents* and not covered by the printed *SCI* are available on-line in file 34.

Research in progress in the biochemical fields may be searched on-line via Lockheed's SSIE Current Research (file 65), covering the latest two fiscal years, and via SDC's file SSIE, covering fiscal year 1974 to the present. The research covered is that sponsored by the U.S. government, and the data base is prepared by the Smithsonian Science Information Exchange, Inc. Complete data, including lengthy summaries, are available on the projects included.

REFERENCES

Bottle, R.T. & Wyatt, H.V. *The Use of Biological Literature.* London: Butterworths, 1967.

Bottle, R.T. & Wyatt, H.V. *The Use of Biological Literature.* London: Butterworths, 1971.

Capitol Systems Group, Inc. *Directory of On-Line Information Resources: A Guide to*

Commercially Available Data Bases. Rockville, Maryland: Capitol Systems Group, Inc., 1978.
Chen, Ching-Chih. *Scientific and Technical Information Sources*. Cambridge, MA: MIT Press, 1977.
Collison, Robert. *The Annals of Abstracting: 1665–1970*. Los Angeles: UCLA, 1971.
Crane, E.J., Patterson, Austin M. & Marr, Eleanor B. *A Guide to the Literature of Chemistry*. New York: John Wiley and Sons, Inc., 1957.
Herner, Saul. *A Brief Guide to Sources of Scientific and Technical Information*. Washington, D.C.: Information Resources Press, 1969.
International Federation For Documentation, *Abstracting Services. Volume 1: Science, Technology, Medicine, Agriculture*. The Hague, Netherlands: FID, 1969.
Koltay, Emery I. *Ulrich's International Periodicals Directory*. 1977–1978. New York: R.R. Bowker Co., 1977.
Malinowsky, H. Robert, Gray, Richard A., & Gray, Dorothy A. *Science and Engineering Literature: A Guide to Reference Sources*. Littleton, CO: Libraries Unlimited, Inc., 1976.
National Federation of Science Abstracting and Indexing Services. *A Guide to the World's Abstracting and Indexing Services in Science and Technology*. Washington, D.C.: NFSAIS, 1963.
Owen, Dolores B. & Hanchey, Marguerite M. *Abstracts and Indexes in Science and Technology. A Descriptive Guide*. Metuchen, NJ: Scarecrow Press, 1974.
Sheehy, Eugene P. *Guide to Reference Books*. Chicago: American Library Association, 1976.

RETRIEVAL OF BIOCHEMICAL INFORMATION BY CHEMICAL STRUCTURE

Phillip Raoul Douville

ABSTRACT. Techniques for retrieval of biochemical information through structure and substructure searching of the practicing biochemist. Commonly applied approaches to searching are reviewed, including Wiswesser Line Notation (WLN). Several of the newer computerized retrieval systems, both private and commercial, are discussed.

An information scientist once commented, half in jest, "the world is in the hands of the indexers." The wisdom of this statement is clearly shown in the case of "false drops" encountered during a computer search. A search through any standard reference work further strengthens the feeling that nothing can quite compete with a properly indexed work. A particular item of information that is not, or cannot be, properly indexed becomes inaccessible, and therefore lost, no matter how many individuals worked to gather it.

The function of any information system (machine or paper) is to store information in a form that makes it readily accessible to the user. When the storage medium for this information system is an electronic computer, the indexing language must be compatible with the machine and, preferably, as efficient as possible; i.e., the language must not demand excessive memory for each indexing symbol. Unfortunately, digital computers would prefer their language to be in binary notation, while humans find it awkward to think in terms of pure numbers. With this language difficulty in mind, "higher order" computer languages (such as FORTRAN, COBOL, PL/1, etc.) have been developed to facilitate the interfacing between human and machines.

Biochemistry has one common denominator, molecular structure, which is an excellent indexing tool and which may be represented by a

---

Phillip Raoul Douville is Associate Professor of Chemistry, Central Connecticut State College, New Britain, CT 06050.

name, a formula, or a notation that represents the three dimensional structure of the molecule. Where the indexing is done with computer retrieval in mind, it is necessary to use computer-compatible notations.

Traditional Manual Methods and their Computerized Relatives

Abstracting journals, such as *Chemical Abstracts* and *Biological Abstracts*, have traditionally used chemical nomenclature and chemical formulae to index specific structures. Where nomenclature is used, the resultant index is organized alphabetically; where formulae are used, the organization is generally by atoms, in some agreed-upon format. For the *Chemical Abstracts* formula indexes, the format for carbon-containing compounds has been to list carbon first, then hydrogen, then the remaining elements in alphabetical order; for compounds not containing carbon, the elements are listed alphabetically.

Traditional indexing methods of nomenclature and formulae have several major disadvantages.

1. To utilize nomenclature, the *correct* name must be known (or be available through cross-references). For many complex substances, such as many of those found in biochemistry, finding the correct name is difficult.

2. To utilize formulae, one must identify a unique formula, or couple the formula with a correct name (since many formulae have multiple names). Again, for many complex substances in biochemistry, this is difficult.

3. The formula or name for the very large biochemical substances may be known, or it may be impossible to apply standard naming and numbering techniques to them, making these substances almost equally impossible to locate.

4. The interest may be in a substructural element of a class of biochemical substances, rather than in a single substance that can be uniquely identified.

To address these difficulties, the approach by traditional abstracting and indexing services has been to use the computer to search by name and formula, utilizing external and internal dictionaries to locate the desired substances.

Chemical Abstracts Service (CAS), for example, developed the capability for handling chemical structures for computer storage and retrieval through its Chemical Registry System (Dittmay, 1976). In this system, each substance is given a machine address in the form of the CAS Registry Number, a number that has no relationship to nomenclature or structure and is therefore unique to the specific substance to which it is attached. This same system, it should be noted, is useful in manual searches, since the CAS Registry Number may be used manually to locate a substance in the *CAS Registry Handbook—Number Section* (CAS, 1977) before searching the *Chemical Substance Index* or the *Formula Index* of *Chemical Abstracts*.

In addition to the Registry Number, a Unique Chemical Registry Record (UCRR) exists in the CAS files for each substance. This UCRR is generated by the following:

a. The Connection Table, a unique computer representation, is dervied by computer from input tables, and describes the sequence of the elements in acyclic connections between ring or acyclic nodes (a node refers to an atom that functions as a branch point). Cyclic or ring nodes are notated by Ring Identifiers (number-letter codes) for the ring systems in which the ring nodes are contained.

b. The stereochemical characteristics of the molecule are indicated by a Text Descriptor. Such descriptors may consist of anywhere from a single letter to the name of a stereoparent molecule, or the descriptor may be a symbol such as (+) or (−) for indication of optical rotation.

c. Isotopically labeled atoms in the structure are indicated by adding a labeling component.

d. A derivative component is added to indicate that the registered substance is a salt or complex of the subtance defined up to this point.

Uses of Computerized Traditional Files

The National Institutes of Health - Environmental Protection Agency Chemical Information System (NIH-EPA CIS) (Heller, 1977) is an on-line service that has adopted the CAS Registry Number and connection tables for machine searches. This service contains data on mass spectra, carbon-13 nuclear magnetic resonance (NMR) spectra, and x-ray diffraction data in a computer file that is accessible, among other possible search modes, by structure or structural fragment (substructure) searches through the use of connection tables in an atom-by-atom search.

Another governmental file that makes use of the CAS Registry Number and chemical formulae for on-line search capability is the Initial

Inventory of the Toxic Substance Control Act (TSCA) (Lockheed Information Services) Chemical Substances Inventory. This file is a non-bibliographic dictionary listing of chemical substances (both toxic and non-toxic) that are in commercial use in the United States.

Similar to TSCA, but with emphasis on the toxic effects of substances, the Registry of Toxic Effects of Chemical Substances of the National Institute for Occupational Safety and Health (NIOSH) also makes use of CAS Registry Numbers to give each substance a unique identification that is totally independent of the nomenclature in use or the search mode for on-line searches. NIOSH applies Wiswesser Line Notation (WLN—to be discussed in some detail below) (Chemical Information Management, 1970; Wiswesser, 1970, 1973) to carry out structure and substructure searches.

Newer Methods of Indexing and Retrieval

To approach the problems of searching noted above, two newer forms of indexing have been developed. Some detail on these and their use follow.

Wiswesser Notation

Beginning with the guiding principle that any new notation system should be written in terms similar to those already in use, Dr. William Wiswesser (Wiswesser, 1970) developed a linear notation that is capable of conveying three-dimensional structural information, using numbers, letters, and spaces for symbols. Wiswesser had two objectives when he developed his notation (WLN):

1. To develop a notation that would serve as an interface between man and machine to facilitate storage and retrieval of three-dimensional information.
2. To develop a notation that could become a new nomenclature for direct non-machine literature searching.

The second objective demands a notation that is relatively easy for the user to learn and use. Unfortunately, no notation that is powerful enough to depict the complex three-dimensional structures found in biological systems is going to be "easy"; however, WLN is written in the sort of notation that is familiar to anyone who has studied chemistry.

In organic structures (in which biochemistry is primarily interested) functional groups are depicted by letters and carbon chains by numbers that refer to the number of carbon atoms in the chain. The list of functional groups covers the majority of symbols used in WLN (Chemical Information Management, 1970) that might be of interest to biochemists. For metals, since they are used less frequently than other elements in biochemical compounds, the symbols are two capital letters enclosed in hyphens.

METAL	SYMBOL
potassium	-KA-
uranium	-UR-
vanadium	-VA-
tungsten	-WO-
yttrium	-YT-

For those occasions when a terminal symbol must represent a non-terminal element, the symbol is enclosed by hyphens. An example here would be $HC1O_2$, which becomes in WLN, Q-G-O.

Examples 1, 2, and 3 show the application to *linear compounds*.

FUNCTIONAL GROUPS	SYMBOL
Br	E (usually terminal)
Cl	G (usually terminal)
$+N\langle$	K
$=NH$	M
$-NH_2$	Z (terminal)
OH	Q (terminal)
phenyl	R (branch symbol)
double bond	U
$-\underset{\underset{O}{\parallel}}{C}-$	V
$=O_2$ (only non-linear, no linear such as CO_2)	W (terminal)
$\rangle C\langle$ (no hydrogens)	X (branch symbol)
$\underset{\parallel}{Y}$ or $\underset{\mid}{CH}$	Y (branch symbol)

Example 1. Ethyl alcohol, C_2H_5OH, becomes Q2 (notice that letters are written before numbers).*

Example 2. The structure
$$\begin{array}{l}CHO\\CH_2\\CH_2\\CHOH\\CO_2H\end{array}$$
becomes VH2YQVQ (note the suppression of the 'H' symbol; the notation is written with the later 'V' first and the earlier 'Q' last).

Example 3.
$$CH_3CH_2CH_2\underset{\underset{Cl}{|}}{\overset{\overset{OH}{|}}{\underset{|}{C}}}\text{---}CH_2\underset{\underset{CH_2}{|}}{\overset{\overset{CH_3}{|}}{CH}}\text{---}\overset{O}{\underset{|}{C}}\text{---}NHCH_2CH_3$$

is translated to ⟶
$$\begin{array}{l}Q\\2\\3X\ 1\ YVM2\\G\end{array}$$

and in final translation becomes→Q2XG3&1Y2&VM2.

Notice the use of the ampersand (&) after 3 and 2. This symbol converts a non-terminal symbol to a terminal symbol, and indicates here that the 3-carbon and the 2-carbon chains are substituents and not part of the main branch.

Molecular structures of interest to the biochemist usually contain one or more *asymmetric carbons*. A naturally occurring member of the amino acid family, (−)threonine (see Example 4) is an example of a substance containing two asymmetric carbons.

The alphanumeric order of preference is "latest" first: earliest: &-/ 0123...ABC... XYZ: latest. The blank space is the earliest of all symbols. Two exceptions to this hierarchy are R=phenyl and H=hydrogen. "R" and "H" are suppressed for indexing purposes to avoid a listing that would include the tremendous number of compounds that could begin with the all too common "R" and "H" symbols.
The notation for the above structure was set up to follow the molecular structure first; then the notation is put into linear form according to the following two rules:
Simplified from rule 6 (Chemical Information Management, 1970):

1. Choose the chain of symbols with the largest number of branch symbols; or
2. choose the chain of symbols with the largest number of notation symbols; and,
3. produce the notation with the latest position.

The branch points are notated according to rule 7 (Chemical Information Management, 1970). The following is simplified from rule 7:

1. Cite branches that contain fewest branch symbols, then
2. cite branches that contain the fewest notation symbols, then
3. cite branches for which the notation has the latest position.

Example 4. O=C-OH   Q
            H₂NCH   V
              NCOH   ⟶   Z1   ⟶   QV1Z1Q1 -BA -L
              CH₃   1Q
                              1

In setting up this notation, the molecule is aligned with the first group listed in WLN on top and the last group listed on the bottom. Substituents that appear to the left of the main branch in the Fischer projection of the molecule are notated after the molecular notation by a space, hyphen, B, those that are oriented right are notated by an A after the space hyphen (or other notation if there is more than one asymmetric carbon as in this case). The last space, hyphen L, stands for the levorotatory compound. The notation for dextro would be space, hyphen, D, and that for meso would be space, hyphen, M. WLN is not yet complete on notations for stereoisomerism, and it is likely that additional terms will be introduced to denote asymmetric centers in the future. For further study on this subject the reader should refer to the Smith-Baker manual (Chemical Information Management, 1970), which is the reference document for all study.

One of the more complex branch points is the *phenyl(R) group*. Substituted benzenes can be coded around the "R" as shown in Example 5 (Chemical Information Management, 1970).

Example 5.

                                1
                                O
                                V   G
                      ⟶   F   R   ⟶   1 VOR CG EF BO1 DVO1
                                V   O1
                                1

Usually locants in a ring are given in lower case letters, but when WLN was first used, computer languages could handle only uppercase letters, making it necessary for Wiswesser to use the space letter combination to represent the lowercase letters. As with linear structures, the main chain of symbols is set up by:

1. Choosing the chain of symbols with the largest number of branch symbols; or
2. choosing the chain with the largest number of notation symbols; then
3. starting at the latest end (in the above example 1VOR would be later than 10VR).

Once the main chain of symbols is chosen and the starting point is determined, the "A" locant is set as that site on the benzene ring where the starting group is attached (here, the 1VO- is the starting group). The first substituent to be named is the substituent with:

1. the *least* number of branch symbols;
2. the least number of notation symbols; and
3. the latest symbol

The Cl⁻ would, then, be the first substituent cited in the notation, and the substituent (G) must be given the lowest possible locant (here, C).

The remaining substituents are cited by the same rules used to choose the first substituent. By these rules, the fluorine atom comes next with the locant "E." Then the next largest substituent is "01," and it comes at the locant "B." Finally, the largest of the substituents to be cited following the "R" symbol is the VO1 at the "D" locant.

Example 6 provides a further example of the substituted benzenes. In

Example 6.

$$\underset{F}{\overset{CH_2CH=CH_2}{\underset{NO_2}{\bigcirc}}} \longrightarrow \underset{F}{\overset{1}{\underset{2}{V}}} R_{NW} \longrightarrow WNR\ DI\ CF\ E2V1$$

this case, the WNR is later than 1V2R, and the "A" locant is placed at the site of the WN group. The first substituent to be cited after the "R" group is I (smallest number of branch symbols; smallest number of notation symbols; and the latest in the alphanumeric hierarchy). The "I" group is situated four positions away from the WN no matter which direction is chosen for numbering, so the locant of the "I" becomes "D". Now it is necessary to decide the direction to be chosen for numbering the entire ring. To do this, it is necessary to set up the two possibilities as they would appear in the notation and decide which would constitute the *earliest* listing of locants.

Again, applying the rules mentioned in the first example, the order of substituents cited after the "R" symbol will be I, F, then 2V1. The two possible directions chosen for numbering the ring from the WN position would produce the locant sequence DCE or DEC. Obviously, DCE is earlier than DEC in the alphanumeric hierarchy, and, therefore, DCE is the sequence of choice.

The above treatment using "R" to depict the ring applies only to benzene rings. *All other ring systems,* six membered or otherwise (see Example 7), are treated by another notation (Chemical Information Management, 1970):

1. The ring structure is enclosed within:
L . . . J for carbocyclic structures (only carbon *in* the ring) and T . . . J for heterocyclic structures (at least one ring carbon atom is replaced by some other atom). Atoms *within* the ring (notation between the L and J or T and J) are listed according to the *lowest* alphanumeric order.

2. Substituents are then listed after the ring symbols (I . . . J or T . . . J) in alphabetic order of their ring locants.

Example 7.

$$\text{structure} \longrightarrow \text{L6V BUTJ EG FG}$$

"L" indicates a carbocyclic system; "6" stands for the six atoms in the ring. The notation symbols following the "6" indicate the ring atoms for which there is special notation and the locants *in* the ring. The final "T" indicates at least two carbons *in* the ring that have four atoms attached to them. Notice that the substituents are notated by a space and letter combination, as was the case for the benzene substituents; unlike the benzene substituents, the substituents here are simply listed in alphabetic order of their ring locants.

Example 8 shows the notation for a heterocyclic case. Notice that the ring segments to be cited in the notation (MYMV) are for consecutive atoms. With the atoms following each other consecutively, it is not necessary to give segment locants, and the first segment cited (as in all cases) is at the "A" position. The "H" symbol with the "E" locant *in* the ring indicates the position of the single carbon *in* the ring attached to four groups.

Example 8.

T 5MYMV EHJ BUM

Of considerable importance to biochemists is the coding of *polymers* (polypeptides, proteins, polysaccharides, etc.). In WLN, repeating units of the polymer are enclosed in slash marks, with asterisks marking the points of attachment in the graphic formula if these points of attachment are known.

An example of a linear homopolymer (similar repeat units that are connected through only two atoms that are not a part of the same ring system) is polybetaalanine (Chemical Information Management, 1970). Graphic formula *c* (see Example 9) read backward, gives the notation with the latest position.

The notation for the polymer then becomes: /*VM2*/

An on-line system that makes use of WLN and has had considerable experience with the limitations of WLN polymer notation is the Index Chemicus Registry System of the Institute for Scientific Information (ISI) (ISI, 1970). It has developed a solution for the difficulty in use of WLN with peptides in which the repeating unit runs more than three amino acids; for such peptides WLN notation becomes inconvenient, and ISI switches to an IC-IUPAC notation in which each of the 26 most

Example 9.

$$(-NH-CO-CH_2CH_2-)_n$$

Setup possible repeat units	Resulting Graphic Formulas
a) $-NH-CO-CH_2-CH_2$	*MV2*
b) $-CH_2NH-CO-CH_2$	*1MV1*
c) $-CH_2CH_2-NH-CO-$	*2MV*
d) $-CO-CH_2-CH_2-NH-$	*V2M*

common amino acid radicals is denoted by a single alphabetic character and other amino acids are denoted by an alphabetic character followed by the special character @. Substituents are coded by two-digit numerical designations. If ISI is still unable to properly code the peptide under consideration, then the peptide is assigned the term PEPT, meaning "peptide not encodable under present rules."

It is beyond the scope of this article to discuss WLN in depth; for a complete discussion of the notation, the reader is referred to the Smith-Baker manual (Chemical Information Management, 1975).

WLN is one of the most versatile notation systems developed to date for indexing of chemical subtances. It is worth noting that even the most difficult structures can be typed on a standard typewriter, with no special symbols needed. The language has been adopted by industrial information systems and reference works and can be conveniently applied to machine searching (both molecular structure and substructure) or hand searching. WLN is a "living" language that is still evolving, as specific applications point up new problems.

Patent Literature

Up to this point, biochemical searches have been considered from the view of the single structure or substructure indexing, with the intention of isolating one substance or substituent and attaining all possible data available. The problem of searching for information on given substances becomes somewhat more complex when it is the patent literature that is being searched. One of the major difficulties in searching patent literature is encountered with the Markush claims or structures. These are patent claims made with variation of one or more structural features of the molecule being patented in order to claim legal right to a maximum number of possible compounds related to the compound or compounds patented. Markush claims can legally bind hundreds of compounds with one patent, and the patent attorney must have access to all possible claims. The biochemist, on the other hand, would be primarily interested in searching patent literature for the compounds actually known or synthesized. A good patent information system must allow access to specific compounds without generating false drops for the multitude of Markush claims that could be present; however, the same system must also allow access to the Markush claims when that is desirable.

To cover problems associated with patent searches, Derwent (Kaback, 1980; Derwent Publications *Instruction Manual #1A*, 1978, *On-Line Users Aid*, 1978) developed a series of fragmentation codes with separate codes for natural products, steroids, dyestuffs, and general chemical structures. The Farmdoc-Agdoc-Chemdoc (see references 10, 11, and 12 for the historical development of these three services) fragmentation code is capable of representing fine structural details, although, in general, it is used to represent such molecular fragments as rings, chains, functional groups, and inorganic components. The chemical information file, which is a part of the on-line World Patents Index (WPI), is accessed by describing either a full or partial structure in terms of the appropriate multipunch codes, and is oriented to the end products of processes under consideration.

The Multipunch Code (originally designed for IBM punch cards) is composed of different sections to deal with the various aspects of searching (Kaback, 1980):

1. The first section introduces the concept of "essential groups" to contend with Markush claims. The code defines groups that must be present in the structure or substructure under consideration, and this code eliminates Markush claims where the group would be only possible and not necessary.

2. This section codes linkages between rings and contains terms that describe the type of each ring and the nature of the linking group.

3. The section on carbon chains is a later addition to the Multipunch Code. The earlier systems (Farmdoc started in 1963) was developed to handle pharmaceutical chemicals and could not cope with the simpler hydrocarbon chains. This code has a limited capability for showing the length of chains.

4. One of the most important codes in the system is the Ring Code. Twenty-four columns of the punch card (a total of 288 coding terms,

actually, since the system is no longer limited to punch cards) are devoted to this code. In 1972, Derwent added Patterson's Ring Index numbers to index ring systems that did not have their own unique position in the Multipunch system. If a given ring system is not found in the Ring Index, Derwent creates its own number system.

5. This section is devoted to functional group codes. Frequently occurring functional groups are coded to show their immediate environment (groups to which functional groups are attached).

At this point, it would be helpful to give an example of how Derwent codes functional groups (Kaback, 1980). The following is an example of an amide in different chemical environments:

> In general, the following hierarchy is used to determine the order of the number codes for different environments; heterocycles before aromatic before alicyclic before aliphatic. A secondary hierarchy: attachment to C of the functional group before attachment to oxygen in ester or nitrogen in amide. Only the highest hierarchical code is to be used for any group.

CODE	FRAGMENT	
481	[heterocycle-C(=O)-NH$_2$]	(heterocycle attached to carbon of amide)
482	[phenyl-C(=O)-N(H)-ø]	(aromatic attached to carbon of amide)
485	[heterocycle-N(H)-C(=O)-ø]	(heterocycle attached to the nitrogen of the amide)
486	[phenyl-N(H)-C(=O)-H]	(aromatic attached to the nitrogen of the amide)

Since the Derwent indexing system has undergone continual evolution from the time of its inception, it is often necessary to use multiple search strategies to cope with the index changes. The on-line WPI file provides for retrieval parameters other than multipunch coding, but these are beyond the scope of this paper.

REFERENCES

1. Dittmar, P.G.; Stobaugh, R.E.; and Watson, C.E. "The Chemical Abstracts Service Chemical Registry System. I. General Design," *Journal of Chemical Information and Computer Sciences*, 1976, *16*, 111–21.
2. Chemical Abstracts Services. *CAS Printed Access Tools, A Workbook*. Columbus, OH: Chemical Abstracts Service, 1977.
3. Heller, S.R.; Milne, G.W.A.; and Feldmann, R.J. "A Computer-Based Chemical Information System," *Science*, 1977, *195*, 253-9.
4. Lockheed Information Services. *TSCA Initial Inventory*, File 52. Palo Alto, CA: Lockheed Information Services.
5. National Institute for Occupational Safety and Health. *Registry of Toxic Effects of Chemical Substances*. Washington, DC: National Institute for Occupational Safety and Health (NIOSH).
6. Wiswesser, W.J., "Chemical Information Management for the 21st Century," *Aldrichemica Acta*, 1973, *6*, 41–9.
7. Wiswesser, W.J., "The Empty Column Revisited," *Computers and Automation*, 1970, *19*, 35–41.
8. Chemical Information Management, Inc. *The Wiswesser Line Formula Chemical Notation (WLN)*. Cherry Hill, NJ: Chemical Information Management, Inc., 1975.
9. Institute for Scientific Information. *Index Chemicus Registry System*. Philadelphia: Institute for Scientific Information (ISI), 1970.
10. Kaback, S.M., "Chemical Structure Searching in Derwent's World Patents Index," *Journal of Chemical Information and Computer Sciences*, 1980, *20*, 1–6..
11. Derwent Publications. *Instruction Manual #1A, CPI/WPI Users Aid*. London: Derwent Publicatons LTD, 1978.
12. Derwent Publications. *On-Line Users Aid*. London: Derwent Publications LTD, 1978

A PARTIAL LIST OF SOME BIOCHEMISTRY AND ORGANIC CHEMISTRY LIBRARY COLLECTIONS

Compiled by Lee Ash, General Editor

Only the names and addresses of these libraries are cited. The list should be helpful as a mailing instrument. Arrangement is geographically by city within state.

ARKANSAS
National Center for Toxicological Research Library, Jefferson, 72079

CALIFORNIA
Bancroft Library, University of California, Berkeley 94720
Biochemistry Library, 430 Biochemistry Bldg., University of California, Berkeley 94720
Biology Library, Univesity of California, 3503 Life Science Bldg., Berkeley 94720
Nutrilife Products Library, 5600 Beach Blvd, Buena Park 90620
Health Sciences Library, University of California, Davis 95616
Beckman Instruments Research Library, 2500 Harbor Blvd., Fullerton 92634
Calbiochem-Bhering Corp. Library, 10933 N. Torrey Pines Rd., La Jolla 92037
Biomedical Library, University of California, Center for Health Sciences, Los Angeles 90024
Chemistry Library, University of California, 4238 Young Hall, Los Angeles 90024
Biological Sciences Research Library, Shell Development Co., Box 4248, Modesto 95352
NASA, Ames Research Center Libraries, Moffett Field 94035
Riker Laboratories (3M) Library, 19901 Nordhoff St., Northridge 91324
Alza Corp. Research Library, 950 Page Mill Rd., Palo Alto 94304
Beckman Instruments Library, 1117 California Ave., Palo Alto 94304
Sylva Company Library, 3221 Porter Drive, Palo Alto 94304
Syntex, USA Library, 3401 Hillview Ave., Palo Alto 94304
Zoecon Corp. Library, 975 California Ave., Palo Alto 94304
Merck & Co. Kelco Div. Library, 8355 Aero Drive, San Diego 92112
IBM Research Library, K25/280, 5600 Cottle Rd., San Jose 95193
Bio-Agricultural Library, University of California, Riverside 92521
McGraw Laboratories Library, Box 11887, Santa Ana 92711

CONNECTICUT
R.T. Vanderbilt Co. Library, 33 Winfield St., East Norwalk 06855
Pfizer, Inc. Library, Eastern Point Rd., Groton 06340
Yale Medical Library, 333 Cedar St., New Haven 06510
Dept of Biochemistry, Yale University, New Haven 06520
Sterling Chemistry Library, Yale University, New Haven 06520
Upjohn Co. Library, 410 Sacketts Point Rd, North Haven 06473

DELAWARE
Agricultural Library, University of Delaware, Newark 19711
Stine Laboratory Library, DuPont de Nemours Co., Box 30, Newark 19711

DuPont Inst. of the Nemours Foundation Library, Box 269, Wilmington 19899
Textile Fibers Library, DuPont de Nemours Co., Experimental Station, Wilmington 19898

DISTRICT OF COLUMBIA
National Biomedical Research Foundation Library, 3900 Rervoir Rd., Georgetown University, Washington 20007
Science & Technology Division, Library of Congress, Washington 20450

FLORIDA
SCM Corporation, Organic Chemicals Library, Box 389, Jacksonville 32201
American Hospital Supply Corp. Library, 1851 Delaware Pkwy., Miami 33152

HAWAII
Pacific Bio-Medical Research Center Library, 41 Ahui St., Honolulu 96813

ILLINOIS
Armak Company Library, 8401 W. 47 St., McCook 60525
Richardson Co. Library, 2701 W. Lake St., Melrose Park 60160
USDA-SEA Northern Regional Research Center Library, 1815 North University St., Peoria 61604
Chemistry Library, University of Illinois, 257 Noyes Laboratory, Urbana 61801

INDIANA
Chemistry Library, Indiana University, Chemistry Bldg., Bloomington 47401
Biochemistry Library, Purdue University, West Lafayette 47907

IOWA
Iowa State University Library, Ames 50011

KANSAS
Willard Library, Kansas State University, Manhattan, 66506
Snyder Memorial Research Foundation Library, 1407 Wheat Rd., Winfield 67156

LOUISIANA
Chemistry Library, Louisiana State University, Baton Rouge 70803

MARYLAND
Eisenhower Library, Johns Hopkins University, Baltimore 21218
National Library of Medicine, 8600 Rockville Pike, Bethesda 20014
White Memorial Library, University of Maryland, College Point 20742

MASSACHUSETTS
Francis A. Countway Library of Medicine (Boston Medical Library/Harvard Medical Library), 10 Shattuck St., Boston 02115
New England Nuclear Corp. Technical Library, 549 Albany St., Boston 02118
Biological Laboratories Library, Harvard University, 16 Divinity Ave., Cambridge 02138
Worcester Foundation for Experimental Biology Library, 222 Maple St., Shrewsbury 01545
Gerstenzang Science Library, Brandeis University, 415 South St., Waltham 02154
E G & A Inc., Mason Research Inst. Library, 57 Union St., Worcester 01608

MICHIGAN
Warner-Lambert/Parke-Davis, Research Library, 2800 Plymouth Rd., Ann Arbor 48106

Lafayette Clinic Library, 951 East Lafayette, Detroit 48207
Warner-Lambert/Parke-Davis Research Library, Joseph Campau at the River, Detroit 48232
Upjohn Co. Corporate Technical Library, 301 Henrietta St., Kalamazoo 49001

MINNESOTA
Pharmacy Library, University of Minnesota, Minneapolis 55455
Biochemistry Library, University of Minnesota, 1445 Gortner Ave., St. Paul 55108

MISSOURI
Petrolite Corporation Library, 369 Marshall Ave., St. Louis 63119
St. Louis College of Pharmacy Library, 4588 Parkview Place, St. Louis 63110

NEW JERSEY
Schering-Plough Corp. Library, 60 Orange St., Bloomfield 07003
J.P. Stevens Co. Library, 141 Lanza Ave., Garfield 07026
Warner-Lambert Co. Library, 170 Tabor Rd., Morris Plains 07950
Color Research Library, DuPont de Nemours Co., 256 Vanderpool St., Newark 07114
Hoffmann-LaRoche, Inc. Library, Nutley 07110
Witco Chemical Corp. Library, 100 Bauer Drive, Oakland 07436
Penick Corp. Library, 215 Watchung Ave., Orange 07050
J.T. Baker Chemical Co. Library, Phillipsburg 08865
Organic & Polymers Division Library, Tenneco Chemicals, Inc., Box 365, Piscataway 08854
American Can Co. Library, Box 50, Princeton 08540
Merck & Co. Research Libraries, Rahway 07065
Ortho Pharmaceutical Corp. Library, U.S. Highway 202, Raritan 08869
Chemical Division Library, Thiokol Corp., 930 Lower Ferry Rd., Trenton 08650
Biovivan Research Inst. Library, 9 South Eighth St., Vineland 08360

NEW YORK
Albert Einstein College of Medicine Library, Morris Park Ave, Bronx 10461
Lucidol Division Library, Pennwalt Corporation, 1740 Military Rd., Buffalo 14240
Cold Spring Harbor Laboratory Library, P.O. Box 100, Cold Spring Harbor 11724
Science Library, Adelphia University, Garden City 11530
Division of Laboratories & Research, Nassau County Dept of Health, 209 Main St., Hempstead 11550
Boyce Thompson Institute for Plant Research, Cornell University Library, Ithaca 14850
FMC Corp. Technical Library, 100 Niagara St., Middleport 14105
American Museum of Natural History Library, Central Park West & 77 St., New York 10024
Biological Sciences Library, Columbia University, New York 10027
Chemistry Library, Columbia University, 454 Chandler Hall, New York 10027
Cornell University Medical College Library, 1300 York Ave., New York 10021
Institute for Muscle Disease Library, 515 East 71 St., New York 10021
Science & Technology Division, New York Public Library, Fifth Ave. & 42 St., New York 10018
Becton, Dickinson Immunodiagnostics Library, Mountain View Ave., Orangeburg 10912
Carlson Library, University of Rochester, Hutchison Hall, River Campus, Rochester 14627
Chemistry Graduate Research Library, Rochester Inst. of Technology, One Lomb Memorial Drive, Rochester 14623
Schenectady Chemicals Library, 2750 Balltown Rd., Schenectady 12309

Wright Research Center Library, Schenectady Chemicals, Inc., 2750 Balltown Rd., Schenectady 12309
Coated Abrasive Division Library, Norton Company, Box 808, Troy 12181
USV Pharmaceutical Corp. Information Services, One Scarsdale Drive, Tuckahoe 10707
Masonic Medical Research Library, Bleeker St., Utica 13501
GE Silicone Products Dept Library, Waterford 12188

NORTH CAROLINA
Zoology Dept. Library, University of North Carolina, Wilson Hall, Chapel Hill 27514
Celanese Fibers Co. Library, Celanese Corporation, Box 32414, Charlotte 28232
Burroughs Wellcome Co. Library, 3030 Cornwallis Rd., Research Triangle Park 27709
National Institute of Environmental Health Sciences Library, P.O. Box 12233, Research Triangle Park 27709
Reynolds Tobacco Co. Science Library, Chestnut at Belews St., Winston-Salem 27102

NORTH DAKOTA
Medical Library, University of North Dakota, Grand Forks 58201

OHIO
Goodyear Tire & Rubber Co. Library, 142 Goodyear Blvd., Akron 44316
PPG Industries Research Library, P.O. Box 31, Barberton 44203
Ferro Chemical Library, P.O. Box 46349, Bedford 44146
Cincinnati Milacron Chemicals Library, West St., Cincinnati 45215
Emery Industries Research Library, 4900 Este Ave., Cincinnati 45232
Science & Industry Dept., Public Library of Cincinnati & Hamilton Cy., 800 Vine St., Cincinnati 45202
Ashland Chemical Co., R&D Library, Box 2219, Columbus 43216
Biological Sciences Library, Ohio State University, 1735 Neil Ave., Columbus 43210
Gilford Instrument Labs Library, 132 Artino St., Oberlin 44074
Diamond Shamrock Corp. Library, P.O. Box 348, Painesville 44077
Lubrizol Corporation Chemical Library, 29400 Lakeland Blvd., Wickliff 44092
Kettering Research Lab. Library, 150 E. South College St., Yellow Springs 45387

PENNSYLVANIA
William H. Rorer, Inc., Library, 500 Virginia Drive, Fort Washington 19034
American Color 7 Chemical Corp. Library, Mt. Vernon St., Lock Haven 17745
Cardeza Foundation Library 1015 Walnut St., Philadelphia 19107
Franklin Institute Library, 20th & The Parkway, Philadelphia 19103
Johnson Research Foundation Library, Richards Bldg., University of Pennsylvania, Philadelphia 19104
Towne Scientific Library, 220 South 33 St., Philadelphia 19104
Science & Technology Dept., Carnegie Library of Pittsburgh, 440 Forber Ave., Pittsburgh 15213
Langley Hall Library, University of Pittsburgh, Pittsburgh 15260
Wyeth Division Library, American Home Products Corp., King of Prussia Rd. & Lancaster Pike, Radnor 19087.
Merck & Co. Research Library, West Point 19486

TENNESSEE
Eastman Kodak Co. Library, Box 511, Kingsport 37662
Buckley Cellulose Corp. Library, Proctor & Gamble Co., 2899 Jackson Avenue, Memphis 38108

TEXAS
Chemistry Library, University of Texas, P.O. Box P. Austin 78712
Celanese Corp. Technical Center Library, Box 9077, Corpus Christi 78408
Wadley Inst. of Molecular Medicine Library, 9000 Hines Blvd., Dallas 75235

VERMONT
Chemistry/Physics Library, University of Vermont, Burlington 05401

VIRGINIA
Dan River, Inc., Research Library, Danville 24541

WASHINGTON
Food, Chemical, & Research Laboratories Library, 4900 Ninth Ave., Seattle 98107

WEST VIRGINIA
Borg-Warner Corp. Library, Box 68, Washington 26181

WISCONSIN
Chemistry Library, University of Wisconsin, 1101 University Ave., Madison 53706
American Bio-Synthetics Corp. Library, 710 W. National Ave., Milwaukee 53204
Pabst Brewing Co. Research Library, 1037 West McKinley Ave., Milwaukee 53205

CANADA
Uniroyal, Ltd, Chemical Division R & D Library, Erb St., Elmira, Ontario N3B 3A3
Uniroyal, Ltd Research Laboratories Library, 120 Huron St., Guelph, Ontario N1H 6N3
Bracken Library, Queen's University, Kingston, Ontario K7L 3N6
Labatt Breweries of Canada Library, 150 Simcoe St., Box 5050, London, Ontario N6A 4M3
Maitland Works Library, DuPont of Canada Ltd, P.O. Box 660, Maitland, Ontario KOE 1PO
Agriculture Canada, Neatby Library, N.W. Neatby Bldg., Rm 3032, Central Experimental Farm, Ottawa, Ontario L1A OC6
Ontario Ministry of Health Library, Box 9000, Terminal A, Toronto, Ontario M5W 1R5
Abbott Laboratories, Ltd, Library, 5400 Cote de Liesse Rd, Montreal, P Q H3C 3K6
Ayerst Laboratories Library, 1025 Laurentien Blvd, St. Laurent P Q H4R 1J6

NOTICE:
NATIONAL LIBRARY OF MEDICINE—
PUBLICATION GRANT PROGRAM
FOR BIOMEDICAL WORKS

The Library's Publication Grant Program provides limited financial support for the preparation and/or publication of biomedical works. Projects that require large-scale or long-term support (beyond a maximum of three years) are not appropriate for the program. Also, support is not provided for the publication of textbooks or other commercially viable products, curriculum materials, initial reporting of research findings, proceedings of meetings, or materials that would have only local interest.

Examples of some of the recent publications resulting from NLM support under provisions of the Medical Library Assistance Act are listed below. *Note:* The National Library of Medicine does not distribute any of these publications; all correspondence regarding their distribution must be directed to the publishers.

Alexander, John T. *Bubonic Plague in Early Modern Russia.* Baltimore, Maryland: The Johns Hopkins University Press, 1980, 385 pp.

Baumel, Julian J., et al., (eds.) *Nomina Anatomica Avium.* London: Academic Press, 1979, 637 pp.

Benzinger, T.H. "The Physiological Basis for Thermal Comfort," In: *Indoor Climate: Effects on Human Comfort, Performance, and Health in Residential, Commercial and Light-Industry Buildings,* edited by P.O. Fanger and O. Valbjorn (Proceedings of the First International Indoor Climate Symposium in Copenhagen, August 30–September 1, 1978). Copenhagen: Danish Building, Research Institute, 1979, pp. 441–474.

Blanco, Richard L. *Physician of the American Revolution: Jonathan Potts.* N.Y.: Garland STPM Press, 1979, 276 pp.

Burlingame, A.L., Baillie, T.A., Derrick, P.J., and Chizhov, O.S. "Mass Spectrometry," *Anal. Chem. Fundamental Reviews,* Vol. 52, 1980, pp. 214R–258R.

Burnham, John C. "The Influence of Psychoanalysis Upon American Culture," In: *American Psychoanalysis: Origins and Development,* edited by Jacques M. Quen and Eric T. Carlson. New York: Brunner/Mazel, Inc., 1978, pp. 52–72.

———. "From Avant-Garde to Specialism: Psychoanalysis in America," *Journal of the History of the Behavioral Sciences,* Vol. 15, 1979, pp. 128–134.

Debus, Allen G. *Robert Fludd and his Philosophical Key.* N.Y.: Science History Publications, 1979. 156 pp.

© 1982 by The Haworth Press, Inc. All rights reserved.

Early Diagnosis of Decompression Sickness. (The Twelfth Undersea Medical Society Workshop). Bethesda, Maryland: Undersea Medical Society, Inc., 1979, 309 pp. (Report No. 7–30–77)

Forbes, Thomas R. "Apprentices in Trouble: Some Problems in the Training of Surgeons and Apothecaries in Seventeenth Century London," *The Yale Journal of Biology and Medicine, Inc.,* Vol. 52, 1979, pp. 227–237.

_____. "By What Disease or Casualty: The Changing Face of Death in London," In: *Health, Medicine and Mortality,* edited by Charles Webster. Cambridge: Cambridge University Press, 1979, pp. 117–129.

Frieden, Nancy M. "Child Care: Medical Reform in a Traditionalist Culture," In: *The Family in Imperial Russia: New Lines of Historical Research,* Edited by David L. Ransel. Urbana: University of Illinois Press, 1978, pp. 236–259.

Grinspoon, Lester and Bakalar, James B. *Psychedelic Drugs Reconsidered.* N.Y.: Basic Books, Inc., 1979, 343 pp.

Grob, Gerald N. "Doing Good and Getting Worse: The Dilemma of Social Policy," *Michigan Law Review,* Vol. 77, No. 3, January–March 1979, pp. 761–783.

_____. "Reflections on the History of Social Policy in America," *Reviews in American History,* September 1979, pp. 293–306.

_____. "Rediscovering Asylums: The Unhistorical History of the Mental Hospital," In: *The Therapeutic Revolution: Essays in the Social History of American Medicine,* edited by Morris J. Vogel and Charles E. Rosenberg. Philadelphia: University of Pennsylvania Press, 1979, pp. 135–158.

O'Neill, Ynez Viole. *Speech and Speech Disorders in Western Thought Before 1600.* Westport, Connecticut: Greenwood Press, 1980, 246 pp.

Patterson, David K. "Health in Urban Ghana: The Case of Accra 1900–1940." *Social Science and Medicine,* Volume 13B, 1979, pp. 251–268.

Rees, Alan M. and Crawford, Susan (comp. and ed.). *Directory of Health Sciences Libraries in the United States, 1979.* Cleveland, Ohio: The Cleveland Health Sciences Library of Case Western Reserve Universty, 1980, 355 pp.

Shilling, Charles W. and Werts, Margaret F. *Physical Methods of Bubble Detection in Blood and Tissues: An Annotated Bibliography with Preliminary Analysis.* Bethesda, Maryland: Undersea Medical Society, Inc., 1979, 85 pp.

Stanbury, John B., and Hetzel, Basil S. *Endemic Goiter and Endemic Cretinism.* N.Y.: John Wiley & Sons, Inc. 1980, 606 pp.

BOOKS OF INTEREST TO SPECIAL COLLECTIONS OF ALL KINDS*

Compiled by Lee Ash, General Editor

(In order not to delay publication of these reviews, those prepared for Volume 1, Number 3 follow this list, since the next issue is to be a large double 1:3/4.)

Guides to Collections and Resources

In the course of my own research in the past quarter, two important guides have come to hand: first, Marian Harman's compilation of *Incunabula in the University of Illinois Library at Urbana-Champaign* (40) published as No. 5 in the series issued on the Robert B. Downs Publication Fund of the University Library and The Graduate School of Library Science a year or so ago. Well over a thousand incunables are listed here, and the Library records 103 otherwise unrecorded in North American collections, according to Goff. The carefully typed entries include full bibliographical descriptions and exemplary notes on provenance as well as other distinguishing features about almost every item. The Index of Titles is particularly helpful for including alternative and analytical titles, etc.; the usual chronological, geographical, and printed indexes are here, and there is a Concordance of the Goff, GKW, Hain, Proctor, Copinger, and Reichling citations. What a treasure Illinois holds for scholarship! A more unusual and brief guide is *Notated Theatrical Dances* (23) recorded in Labanotation, Benesh Movement Notation, Eshkol-Wachman Movement Notation, in New York, London, and Holon, Israel, respectively. The largest and most accessible are the Labanotation group in the archives of the Dance Notation Bureau in New York. The guide also includes a list of "Institutions Using DNB Reconstruction (Labanotation) and Licensing Services, 1970-79." This is a helpful pamphlet giving information otherwise nearly impossible to find.

---

*Bibliographical citations by author, keyword, or subject follow this review article. The number of the citation in the list appears in the text. Prices are listed when known.

The contributions to material culture by German-American and German-Canadian groups through recent centuries are located and described in *Museums, Sites, and Collections of Germanic Culture in North America* (31), compiled by Margaret Hobbie, a very full and efficiently annotated directory of German immigrant culture in the United States and Canada. When known, entries (arranged by state and province) include name, address, telephone, director of staff, description of collections, dates covered, catalogued status, hours, and lending policy. A complete collection of similar directories of other cultures—of which odds and ends of greater or lesser competency exist—would be very useful. Another type of community is dealt with in Robert S. Fogarty's *Dictionary of American Communal and Utopian History* (20), one of the very best of a few similar modern works, most of which are essentially comparative studies. Fogarty's book is devoted to well written, balanced biographical entries, followed by comparably effective descriptions of named communities, then a much longer Appendix, "Annotated List of Communal and Utopian Societies, 1787–1919," by Otohiko Okugawa. There is a fine "Communal History in America," a bibliographical essay, with a selected bibliography, and a good index. Throughout the book, "selected works" and "sources" are cited for most articles. *Utopias: the American Experience* (72), edited by Gairdner B. Moment and Otto F. Kraushaar, expands on many of the facts and incidents mentioned in the previously noted reference book—all the way to the Jonestown tragedy—in essays by specialists, presented in the American Bicentennial year under the auspices of Goucher College and Johns Hopkins University.

Two smaller libraries have done highly specialized guides to collections in their charge. Manhasset Public Library, New York, has compiled a list of *Books* on Books (8), a good checklist for general medium-sized public library collections. The list is made up from a collection of generous annual donations from the Library's "Friends" group and other sources, now over 250 titles. The Norris Medical Library, Health Sciences Campus, University of Southern California, Los Angeles, has issued a less attractive *Bibliography of Spanish Medical Books* (4), compiled by Edward Emke, and edited by Robin E. Wagner. There are descriptions of 319 items, mostly of the 18th and 19th century, mostly translated from English and European authors. The collection will probably be of greatest use to Spanish-speaking students. Many of the foreign titles have also been translated into English.

Directories and Indexes

The New York Metropolitan Reference and Research Library Agency (METRO) has compiled its fourth edition of the *METRO Directory of Members, 1980/81* (46), which is of interest and somewhat helpful even though limited by the membership's sometimes exclusive rules. About 100 libraries' names, addresses and telephone numbers, personnel access and services, subject strengths, and special collections are noted. The subject index to the last two items is—as is so often true—of limited value, being far from a good analysis (or even listing) of specialties noted in the descriptions. For example, the New York Zoological Society has real subject strengths in "vertebrate zoology, captive [animal] management, veterinary medicine, conservation, and rare books in natural history, mainly zoology," but only veterinary medicine and zoology are indexed; indeed there is no index entry at all for Conservation collections in New York! Nor are there cross-references in the index. Far superior is *Australian Scientific Societies and Professional Associations,* 2d Edition (3), edited by Ian A. Crump, and though of limited use, perhaps, in this country, it will be helpful to concerned researchers in many fields and in the preparation of mailing lists. Entries are very informative and more complete than those of most directories, and the subject index is quite thorough; there are indexes of initials and acronyms, a title index to Publications of the organizations (most useful), and an Awards index.

Writer's & Photographer's Guide to Newspaper Markets (75) lists over 150 newspapers that use freelance writings and/or photographs, far more than one finds in the *Writer's Market* or other sources. Coverage is geographically spotty but will surely improve as new editions succeed one another. Names and addresses of publications are given, with information about the newspapers, what they are interested in having, pay, etc.

A major new publication from Gale is *The Directory of Directories* (26), edited by James M. Ethridge—with a usual supplementary service called *Directory Information.* The sampler sent for review includes sections from the fifteen classified main subject sections, and the complete title and analytical subject indexes. There can be no doubt that this comprehensive listing is the most complete and informative one ever compiled, the scope of the main entries filled with pertinent descriptive information. This is a major reference source. Similarly, but of world-wide interest and limited to library information, *World Guide to Libraries,*

5th Edition (47), is a tremendous volume, listing all kinds of libraries, their correct addresses, telephone (Telex and telegraphic codes), date of founding, name of director, departments, volumes, interlibrary loan participation, etc., etc.; there is also a valuable "Code List [initialisms] of Library Associations". So thorough is the book that three libraries are listed in Doha, Qatar, and fifty-two in Singapore—national, university and college, professional school, government, religious, business, other special, and public.

Dictionaries, Encyclopedias, Atlases, and Other Reference Books.

I am still testing the only dictionary noticed in this issue of *Special Collections*, the new *Oxford American Dictionary* (25A), and so far I have enjoyed its very simple and generally adequate definitions. I am satisfied that it distinguishes "biweekly" from "semiweekly," and hyphenates all "self-" entries; my greatest shudder comes from "picture (pik-chur)," though "accessories" is not—as on TV—"assessories" and *is* "aK..." While there are four-letter words, none of them will horrify school or library boards. It seems to be an entirely safe and fair book, even hippies "using (or thought to be using) hallucinogenic drugs."

In a single alphabet, John E. Findling has written his *Dictionary of American Diplomatic History* (1), and his excellent Introduction describes his criteria for inclusion or exclusion very carefully. Most of the book consists of biographical entries which emphasize diplomatic activities of importance; the subject entries are many and include such entries as Alaska Purchase, Cairo Conference, NSC-68, and Virginius Episode. Various helpful appendixes include a Chronology of American Diplomatic History; Key Diplomatic Personnel; Initiation Suspension, and Termination of Diplomatic Relations; and Locations of Manuscript Collections and Oral Histories; and an index.

In days of energy shortages it might not seem that Richard Crashaw deserves the time that went into computerization for *A Concordance to the English Poetry of [his works]* (22), compiled by Robert M. Cooper and programmed by Sundaran Swetharanyam. This may not be a kind remark to make about Mr. Cooper's hard work and interests but for the large amount of money that the book costs, few scholars and fewer libraries will likely derive much advantage from the amount of effort that has gone into this and most of the recent years' abundance of similar concordances. Entries include key words, complete line, title or short title, line number, date of poem in Martin's Oxford edition, page numbers in both Martin's and Williams' standard edition. More impressive for its keen scholarship and peripheral reference use is Betsy Erkkila's *Walt Whitman Among the French* (74), analyzing the influences of French writers on Whitman (and some others), and his, in turn, on Rimbaud, Gide, Claudel, and more, on a variety of schools of modern literature and art. *Precipitous City:* the Story of Literary Edinburgh (27), by Trevor Royle, is not as successful in its purpose as some earlier books on the same subject. It is, nevertheless, wholly readable and enjoyable, and explains the sources of many historical and literary allusions. It should not be neglected.

Still evaluating books of literary criticism and their ilk, the very full name and title index found in Paul Brooks' *Speaking for Nature (57)*, tells how literary naturalists, from Thoreau to Rachel Carson, have shaped America and makes for interesting insights into the bibliography and historiography of natural history. While on the subject of natural history and publications useful for reference, we should consider the following works for special collections. First in importance is *The Red Notebook of Charles Darwin* (24), so fully and capably edited, with an Introduction and Notes by Sandra Herbert. Published now for the first time, the illustrated notebook covers mid-1836 to mid-1837, observations on the last lap of the Beagle voyage, and intimates suspicions of the evolutionary process. It is one of the most important and basic volumes of Darwiniana of recent years. This is a book for all collections on the biological sciences. Another careful observer of nature is Peter Scott, son of the Antarctic explorer and one of the finest professional painters of natural history of our generation. Some of his best paintings, of considerable reference value, are in his *Observations of Wildlife* (58), along with his autobiographical story. It is a story, excitingly illustrated, that will be welcome in all natural history and public library collections.

Before leaving natural history, I want to include notice of a very informal and friendly publication (though some issues are very worth preserving in any library), *New York City Notes On Natural History* (60), which includes notes on Indians, fossils, geography and geology, natural history, and the history of the metropolitan region authoritatively. The editor/publisher, Sidney Horenstein, is a member of the scientific staff of the American Museum of Natural History and teaches at Hunter College.

Palebotany is one of the more isolated and specialized sciences, and very little has been written about its history, so Professor Henry N. Andrews' *The Fossil Hunters: In Search of Ancient Plants* (63) will quickly become a reference tool for all who do historical research in botany, paleontology, and geology. Not only is the book a biographical compendium, but it is also a critique of particular works by the authors who are discussed. An apt pen and Andrews' thorough scholarship should mark this book for one of the prizes awarded for science and literary merit.

This brings me to a clutch of current McGraw-Hill books concerning hallucinogens. Two of them are about plants and the third about the synthetic drug, LSD. Most important, R. Gordon Wasson's latest contribution (Number 7 of his Ethnomycological Studies) is *The Wondrous Mushroom: Mycolatry in Mesoamerica* (33), which is a sound and attractive paperbound issue of the expensive DeLux Limited Edition of 401 copies, illustrated, but without colorplates. Wasson's works have opened new areas of psychiatric, pharmacological, ethnobotanic, and anthropological research. They have had a profound impact on the modern development of these sciences, and scholars are revising old histories based on hitherto insufficient evidence in terms of Wasson's researches. Wasson is the preeminent authority on the use of psychoactive mushrooms in the cultures of India, Greece, Siberia, North and Central America. I believe that his works are destined to become classics of psychiatry, natural history, anthropology, and mycology. Another strikingly important contribution to the literature of botanical hallucinogens and anthropology is Richard Evans Schultes' and Albert Hofmann's *Plants of the Gods: Origins of Hallucinogenic Use* (32), a necessary reference work for all public and academic libraries and many special collections. These two authorities—the Director of the Harvard Botanical Museum (as well as Manglesdorf Professor of Natural Sciences), and the discoverer of LSD—have compiled a nearly definitive reference book. They have included explication of the origins and use of different mind-altering drugs throughout the world, while emphasizing, without sensational references, warnings about their unknown and frequently dangerous effects. The fine illustrations enhance understanding of this excellent book. Additionally, Albert Hofmann has writen *LSD: My Problem Child* (31A), which tells the story of his isolation of LSD, his first experimental use on himself, other early users, and later events in the drug culture, with some comment on Timothy Leary, and on the future of hallucinogens. Collections emphasizing cookery as well as botany will be delighted with *Herbs and Spices: the Pursuit of Flavor* (35), edited by Waverley Root, which is a new kind of textual format in herb books, explaining how to choose herbs and spices, grow them, cook with them, and enjoy them. The color-illustrated "Plant Lexicon" is one of the easiest to use, and most informative, I have found.

The Royal Facts of Life (34), by Mark Hansen, treats of the consequences of biological and medical problems of royalty and their mix with politics in 16th-century Europe. Anyone doing biographical or historical research on the period is likely to be led to new ideas by this remarkably intuitive but mostly factual book about birth, childhood, marriage, sex, health, and death among the Tudors, Stewarts, Valois, Hapsburgs, and others. *Death in Literature* (25), edited by Robert F. Weir, describes how the common man, as well as royalty, has been affected by The Inevitable as described in writings from ancient to modern authors who have considered just that—its inevitability; personification; personal views of the dying; death scenes; children, youth, and death; murder; suicide; funeral and burial customs; bereavement; and immortality. Certainly provocative considerations and, though it is not a reference book, effective use can be made of if by the reference librarian. Similarly, reference use will be found for the very intelligent analysis of *Mind and Madness in Ancient Greece* (66), by Bennett Simon, M.D., who, as a classical scholar and psychiatrist, examines the ancient roots of modern psychiatry as described in such sources as the Homeric Epics, Greek tragedy, Hippocrates, and Aristotle—all in psychoanalytical contexts. This is a theme continued, and expanded to modern literature in Lillian Feder's *Madness in Literature* (51), citing not only ancient literature but bringing her examples to date through the ages to Ginsberg, Roethke, Berryman, and Plath.

Transitionally, from some medical books to the arts, let me note a good two-volume reference set, Medicine and Stamps (65), edited by R.A. Kyle, M.D. and M.A. Shampo, keyed to Scott's Standard Postage Stamp Catalogue. This is a collection and revision, with additions, of John A. Mirt's filler pieces in the Journal of the AMA, but with many more illustrations.

On to the arts! Earliest, in chronological interest, is Marc Drogin's *Medieval Calligraphy: Its History and Technique* (14), the only modern book which, comprehensively, gives sufficient, clearly described, brilliantly photographed, and clearly reproduced examples of both major and minor hands along with explicit directions for writing them. Not only calligraphers need this book, but it is also a new and exciting approach to the study of palaeography. As such, it should be in any collection of calligraphic examples or wherever examples of early manuscripts are held.

Among the few books on furniture received this quarter is a fine Dover reprint—one of Dover's usual quality books—of an unabridged and unaltered republication of the limited edition of Nancy McClelland's *Duncan Phyfe and the English Regency* (29), a standard reference work difficult to find since its publication in 1939.

Two fantastically beautiful art books have come from Princeton University, which has become a leading publisher of the genre in the past few years. *William Blake, Printmaker* (7), by Robert N. Essick, is the most scholarly and unique study of the artistic and personal influences that created the individuality of the artist/craftsman, Blake. The book describes his experiments with different techniques, and the commercialization of some of his enterprises. There is, throughout, deep analysis of Blake's personality as related to his art forms. One of the appendixes is a catalogue of states and impressions of Blake's three political prints of 1793–1794, which I do not think has been offered elsewhere. There is a colored frontispiece and nearly 250 handsomely reproduced black-and-white plates. The other superb book from Princeton is the two-volume set of Julius S. Held's long-anticipated opus, *The Oil Sketches of Peter Paul Rubens: a Critical Catalogue* (68). The first volume is the definitive work on the subject and not only a descriptive catalogue of some 500 paintings—giving location, title, date, physical description, provenance, literature citations, and bibliographical references—but a wonderful guide to iconographic representation. The second volume reproduces 24 paintings in color and over 500 in black-and-white. The bibliography is stupendous!

Somewhat less pretentious is Cornell University Press's *The Story of Modern Art* (2), by Norbert Lynton. This is a solid and interesting book for the curious reader and for reference use. The international phenomenon of the rise of modern art is made fully intelligible through a well-written text and an absolutely great selection of reproductions—85 in color and over 200 others, all clearly printed and of sufficiently good size (some full-page) to be interesting. This becomes my desk book for reference about the subject. Cornell has also sent Gareth Rees' *Early Railway Prints* (67), scenes and pictures of British railways from 1825 to 1850. Print collectors and those who are always called "railroad buffs" will be interested in this volume which, though highly specialized in both subject areas, is attractive and stimulating. While my interest in prints is deep, it has not included railway prints, but I learned a lot from this book, and now I know more about railway prints and trains that I would have guessed I might care about. A good book for reference and browsing.

Architectural buffs, and there are many, will be particularly interested in Mary Cable's nostalgic volume, *Lost New Orleans* (59), about a city that has had great devastation in the past and again in recent years. Mark Twain and Frederick Law Olmsted loved New Orleans as have thousands of others, and the history of the city is appealingly told, often referring to important historic incidents and dramatic happenings. The illustrations, particularly those showing buildings, are excellently selected. This is the story of a city that has greatly influenced American social, political, and intellectual history.

I do not believe that there has been sufficient notice given to the reprinting of the long-unavailable *Practical Guide to American Nineteenth Century Color Plate Books* (19), by Whitman Bennett, covering publications of 1800 to 1900 including at least three colored plates. This is an essential reference tool for the art library and the antiquarian bookseller or collector, and I wish to help notice the reprint here.

Music libraries of academic status will surely be anxious to acquire Anthony Newcomb's complete study of *The Madrigal at Ferrara, 1579–1597* (56), Number Seven in the Princeton Studies of Music series. The first volume of Text presents a wholly new revision of our concept of the Renaissance's presentation of certain musical forms. The second volume of Musical Examples gives the words, translation, and clearly printed musical transcriptions of over 25 madrigals unavailable in modern editions. *Church Music: an International Bibliography* (56A), by Richard Chaffey von Ende, includes books principally of the western world and, mostly, of the Christian Church, with some exceptions. There are nearly 5500 bibliographical references classified under dozens and dozens of subjects, denominations, and national anthems, with an index to authors, editors, and compilers.

Since we all pose as protectors of the Muse of History, it is difficult to think of the special collections librarian—or any librarian—who would not benefit from reading *The Past Before Us* (36), edited for the American Historical Association by Michael Kammen. This is a book of historiography that actually explains how history is written and the many factors that affect its interpretation in written form and in different kinds of studies. The contributors are all cogent scholars, and a superior job of editing has produced an invaluable guide to a subject we should all understand better than we librarians have in the past. An additional reading that supplements the Kammen volume is found in Lewis E. Saum's *The Popular Mood of Pre-Civil War America* (37), a very difficult subject to write about. The book is a different and exciting study of attitudes and history, but most interesting are Saum's provocative historiographic essays: the Introduction, and the appendix, "Some Thoughts Regarding Procedure, Related Scholarship, and Sources." A new *Oral History Evaluation Guidelines* (61), report of the 1979 Wingspread Conference is considered "a major step towards improvement of the oral history work being done in the United States," and the pamphlet ought to be in every library in the nation. It is definitive, clear, and necessary to understanding this relatively new method for the transcription of history.

Some unusual customs, hard to search out in the reference department, are described in Jeffrey's L. Lant's amusing but helpful book, *Insubstantial Pageant: Ceremony and Confusion at Queen Victoria's Court* (17), describing some unbelievable bits of etiquette, respect, celebration, dining and drinking rules, problems of dress and accoutrement, etc. "Twas a mad, mad world, and we have inherited much of it!"

An exciting announcement from the University of Toronto Press is a decision by the Social Sciences and Research Council of Canada to award the Press a $3.5 million grant to support research and production of a three-volume *Historical* Atlas of Canada (15) over a period of six years.

Bibliographies and Special Booksellers' Catalogues

Four interesting author bibliographies have come to my desk. First was an exhibit of *William Faulkner's Gifts of Friendship: Presentation and Inscribed Copies From the Faulkner Collection of Louis Daniel Brodsky* (28), one of the most unusual single modern author collections, held at the University of Mississippi, the illustrated catalogue based upon a selection exhibited August-September 1980. Another modern author's interests are represented in Donald Gallup's catalogue of an exhibition he arranged for the Summer of 1980, being *Carl Van Vechten, 17 June 1880–17 June 1980: a Centenary Exhibition of Some of His Gifts to Yale* (73). Third is an important volume, *Carson McCullers: a Bibliography* (50), by Adrian M. Shapiro and others, describing all editions of her books and other first appearances, adaptations, and English-language foreign editions; the second part of the book is an annotated bibliography of books, and parts of books, periodical articles, and reviews of her works; there are also author and subject indexes. This is, by far, the best bibliography of McCullers. Fourth, *Gabriel Garcia Marquez: an Annotated Bibliography, 1947–1979* (30), compiled by Margaret Eustella

Fau, which one hopes will make this Colombian novelist and journalist's works more accessible to a public that knows him best through his remarkable *One Hundred Years of Solitude*, published in 1967 and issued in English in 1970. Naruda called it "the greatest revelation in the Spanish language since Don Quixote." Surely translations of more than the few stories listed in English are called for.

Is *The International Sherlock Holmes* (39) an author bibliography? Well, at any rate Ronald Burt DeWall has compiled a companion volume to *The World Bibliography of Sherlock Holmes and Dr. Watson, 1887–1971*, the new volume providing complete listings, with annotations or descriptions, of Sherlockiana appearing from even before 1971 to 1978. Over 6000 new entries (bringing the two volumes to over 12,000 numbered entries describing over 20,000 items). Surely only Holmes himself could find more!

There is no reason for bibliographies to be physically unattractive, which is proved again by James R. Cox's *Classics in the Literature of Mountaineering and Mountain Travel* (55), an annotated bibliography of especially important pieces in the Francis P. Farquhar collection of mountaineering literature at the UCLA Library. This beautiful volume, designed by Grant Dahlstrom and printed at The Castle Press, Pasadena, is an edition limited to 500 copies. The 110 classics date from Gesner, 1543 (in the Grabhorn Press edition of 1937) to Hornbein's *Everest: the West Ridge*, 1965. A delightful and very informative bibliography.

Few scholars have sufficient competency, when facing the ever-increasing literature of their subjects, to dare something like Eleanor Blum's *Basic Books in the Mass Media* (21), but having survived the experience, Ms. Blum has produced a fine 2nd Edition of her very helpful "annotated, selected booklist covering general communications, book publishing, broadcasting, editorial journalism, film, magazines, and advertising." Here is a retired library school professor (Illinois) who is one of the most competent among us.

Two bibliographies of Latin American interest are David P. Werlich's *Research Tools for Latin American Historians: a Select, Annotated Bibliography* (4), 1347 reference works arranged in special classes—e.g., Bibliographies, Newspapers, Theses & Dissertations, Official Publications, Libraries, Maps & Atlases, Book Reviews, etc., etc., and by twenty individual nations. Annotations are succinct and pointed, and emphasize special features. There are indexes of main entries and of selected topics. This is an indispensable guide. The nearly 11,000 items listed in Ronald Hilton's book, *A Bibliography of Latin America and the*

Caribbean: the Hilton Library (43), is a straight unannotated author listing but not nearly as useful as the Werlich volume with its classified and annotated contents. Of course the book has a different purpose and is far more inclusive. It will be used mostly to verify entries and for interlibrary loan.

The Invisible Empire (42), by William H. Fisher, is a very competently annotated bibliography of a dread organization, the Ku Klux Klan. This is a most complete bibliography, an accumulation of the bulk of English-language material about the Klan to 1978. Since the character of the Klan changed in the 20th century, the earlier material makes up the first part of the book. Both parts are divided into three sections: Dissertations, Manuscripts/Archives, Government Documents; Monographs; Articles. The annotations are carefully analytical, and there are author and subject indexes. Entries all refer specifically to the Klan only, so more should not be expected.

Plot summaries are provided for nearly 900 short stories in *The American Indian in Short Fiction: an Annotated Bibliography* (41), by Peter G. Beidler and Marion F. Egge. Listing the numbered stories alphabetically by author, title, and published source, there are supplementary indexes by tribes and subject key words. The informative annotations help to answer a variety of questions about this genre of short story and suggest many topics for further research. It is unforunate that the subject index is not better defined (broken-down, that is), since over 150 item citations numbers under "Cultural Misunderstanding" and more than 200 for "Animal" are discouraging leads. After the Indians it is easy to turn one's attention to the *War Story Guide: an Annotated Bibliography of Military Fiction* (54), a long-needed compilation of nearly 4000 stories by Myron J. Smith, Jr., with an appreciative Foreword by General Mark Clark. In three parts—Before the 20th Century, the 20th Century, and Chronicles Covering More Than One Period, Part One is subdivided geographically, Part Two by time periods since 1900. There are author and title indexes, and an index of Battles, Wars, and Warrior Index. The annotations are simple and wholly uncritical.

A number of attractive booksellers' catalogues, some of which also serve as at least partial bibliographies, appeared here in this quarter. I am sorry to have heard recently from Walter Reuben (71) that his fine recent series, which have included offerings of long lists of "Translations of American and British Literature, will not be continued; these are lists of real reference value to collectors and scholars. Those of us who have them will continue to find them useful. *Books On the Sea* (69) is a recent catalogue of The Current Company and itself a "collector's item."

Opening with a section of The America's Cup, there are successive sections on Islands, Literature of the Sea, Naval History, Seamanship & Navigation, Ships & Shipping, Voyages & Travels, Yachts & Yachting, etc. — nearly 600 items. Much of this catalogue will have been sold when my note appears; the catalogue's appeal, however, with its scholarly and interesting annotations, will continue. *John Steinbeck: a Collection of Books & Manuscripts Formed by Harry Valentine of Pacific Grove, California* (70) is a handsome catalogue of books for sale by Bradford Morrow, Bookseller of Santa Barbara. Published in an edition of 2500 copies bound in printed wrappers and 250 in boards, this 154-page illustrated book offers 700 lots at both high and low prices. Importantly, this excellent volume is a supplement and corrective to the Goldstone and Payne *Bibliography*, and worthy of standing beside it. *Catalogue Twenty-Five: Bibliography* (11) by Oak Knoll Books—among my favorite booksellers—contains an author-subject alphabet of more than 2000 items carefully described and overwhelmingly exciting to anyone who collects Books About Books; also *Catalogue 26, Books About Books*, 513 items. Attention should be brought to William Reese's second catalogue, *Americana* (12) with its variety of unusual books and ephemera from the 17th to the 20th century. This neat catalogue, printed from typescript, contains some of the most fascinating annotations I have read this year. For a very small cost, only $3, a series of three catalogues on *The Arctic* (10) by Ontario's specialist dealer, J. Patrick McGahern, will add to the reference resources of any library. Strictly an author/subject list, there are 1251 items. Annotations are infrequent, but the citations are accurate, and the breadth of the collection is unusual.

Ten years of fine printing by Barry Moser's Pennyroyal, in Northampton, Mass., are celebrated in a charming pamphlet, limited to 1000 copies, which includes two lovely woodcuts (64). And another brief note: Frank J. Anderson now conducts a column entitled, "The Private Printers' Patch" in the bimonthly *Briarpatch*, subscription information from Box 2482, Davidson, North Carolina.

Administration of Collections

Collection Development and Management at Cornell (44), by Hendrik Edelman and Dan C. Hazen, is an interim report on activities of the Cornell University Libraries' Project for Collection Development and Management, 1977–79. It is one of the best-thought-out studies of a variety of approaches to some of the large library's problems that became difficult in the Sixties and crucial in the Seventies. Space planning and the philosophy of collection development at Cornell are closely related to the challenges described in Osburn's book (following here) and represent a series of "practical" solutions though many are still being studied and tested.

Tremendously important to the future of librarianship everywhere in this country, Charles B. Osburn's cogent *Academic Research and Library Resources* (48) examines changing patterns in America. While describing what has happened in the somewhat indifferent past and recent years, he explains—"warns" might be a better word—the extent to which patterns of research have adopted new and very different concepts, techniques, and purposes. This is one of the most exciting books about the intellectual content of librarianship since Pierce Butler codified his theories of the humanistic tradition in libraries some fifty years ago. Another thought-provoking publication of theoretical concepts that should be of interest to authors, publishers, librarians, and educators, is *The Audience for Children's Books* (18), being remarks and comments at a symposium sponsored by The Center for the Book and the Children's Literature Center, held at the Library of Congress in March 1979. I found Barbara Rollock's remarks on "The [Changed and Changing] Audience for Children's Books" especially convincing and valuably informative.

The fourth edition of A.M. Lewin Robinson's *Systematic Bibliography* (6) offers some new illustrations of bibliographical layouts, and continues as a leading text for introducing the subject to both British and American student assistants and beginning librarians.

I am never very enthusiastic about texts on literary criticism; one book, however, has provided fascinating information and new approaches that will benefit any librarian who is a reader. Marjorie Boulton's *The Anatomy of Literary Studies: an Introduction to the Study of English Literature* (49) is a friendly and new approach to understanding why literary criticism is important and what its effective components are. It is thoroughly enjoyable reading which "emphasizes humility and honesty as essential qualities of scholarship and urges a sense of fun when studying the [any!] subject." Censorship as a tool of intellectual criticism is depicted in L.B. Woods' *A Decade of Censorship in America* (16) which demonsrates the widely present threat to classrooms and libraries from 1966 to 1975 (and in still ongoing years). Quantitative data, lists of books censored, of sources of censorship, reasons for it, etc., are presented and show librarians and educators the clear and present danger toward which much stronger reaction is required as the nation turns to a new conservatism.

The new Technical Leaflet 131 of the American Association for State and Local History, *Manuscript Collections: Initial Procedures and Policies* (52), by David H. Hoober, Curator of Manuscripts, Arizona Historical Society, gives excellent advice for all persons who might be concerned, and it would be my preferred suggestion for a guide that all of us who are "experts" can suggest to less experienced inquirers. Its twelve pages will also give student assistants in manuscript collections a good idea of what they are doing and why.

Already widely accepted as the best guide to handling many special problems that arise in every library, Alfred H. Lane's *Gifts and Exchange Manual* (45) has leaped into position as one of the most useful books in the literature of library administration, and its pertinency for special collections librarians will be immediately recognized. A long-needed "how to" book, it does not neglect the philosophies of exchanges and gifts while it explains and emphasizes techniques for handling both classes of materials. Not least, the section on the disposition of unwanted gifts or other holdings is very helpful. Useful appendixes include IRS guidelines, a list of appraisers, the ACRL Statement on Appraisals, gift policy statements, and sample forms. Both large and small libraries will benefit from study of this excellent book.

As an aside, collectors and librarians with interests in T.E. Lawrence should all be aware of Item 536 in the Sotheby Park Bernet catalogue for its 21/22 July 1980 sale of an apparently unpublished 1924 letter to an old companion-in-arms, Major W.F.Stirling, "about the background to, authenticity of and influence upon *Seven Pillars of Wisdom*..." and other facts about his life. Lawrence wrote, "If people read it as history: - then they mistake it..." The note is much fuller but reference to it and the letter are essential for the historian and literary critic considering *The Seven Pillars*...

Lastly, another British item not sufficiently well known to research libraries in this country is *British Library News* (13), of which about sixty numbers have appeared. It is, of course, a brief release from the British Library (still more familiar to many of us as the BM), describing major happenings, staff and administrative activities, collection developments, and the very important and often unusual new publications of the BL. It is distributed monthly free of charge, by the Press and Public Relations Section.

BOOKS RECEIVED

1. *American Diplomatic History, Dictionary of,* by John E. Findling. xviii, 622 pp. Westport, Ct: Greenwood Press, 1980. $39.95.
2. *Art, Modern, The Story of,* by Norbert Lynton (A Phaidon Book). Profusely Illus., incl. Color. 382pp. Ithaca: Cornell University Press, 1980. $35.00.
3. Australian Scientific Societies and Professional Associations. Ed. by Ian A. Crump. 2d Edn, [399 organizations described]. v, 226pp. Melbourne: Information Service, Commonwealth Scientific and Industrial Research Organization, 1978 [distr. by ISBS, Inc., P.O. Box 555, Forest Grove, Or., 971168. $10.00.
4. (BIBLIOGRAPHY, LATIN AMERICAN). Werlich, David P. *Research Tools for Latin American Historians.* (Garland Reference Library of Social Science, Vol. 60). xvi, 269pp. N.Y.: Garland Publishing Co., 1980. $30.00.
5. (BIBLIOGRAPHY, MEDICAL). Emke, Edward. Bibliography of Spanish Medical Books. Ed. by Robin E. Wagner [319 items]. 61pp. Los Angeles: Norris Medical Library, University of Southern California [2025 Zonal Avenue, Zip 90033], 1979. Inquire.
6. *Bibliography, Systematic:* a Practical Guide to the Work of Compilation, 4th Edn, Rev., by A.M. Lewin Robinson: With an Additional Chapter by Margaret Lodder. 135pp. N.Y.: K.G. Saur, 1979. $18.75.
7. *Blake, William, Printmaker,* by Robert N. Essick. Colored Frontispiece & 236 Black & White Illus. 283pp. Princeton: Princeton University Press, 1980. $50.00.
8. (BOOKS ABOUT BOOKS). Manhasset Public Library, N.Y. *Books On Books:* a Special Collection. 19pp. N.Y. [Zip 11030], 1980. Inquire.
9. (BOOKSELLER'S CATALOGUE). E.P. Goldschmidt. Catalogue 160: *Continental Printed Books, 1480–1700* [251 items]. Illus., incl. Color Plate. 85pp. London: E.P. Goldschmidt [64 Drayton Gardens, SW10 9SB], 1980. Inquire.
10. (BOOKSELLER'S CATALOGUE). McGahern, J. Patrick. *Catalogue 38: The Arctic* [3 parts; 1251 items]. 56pp. Ottawa, Ont. [763 Bank St Zip K1S 3V3]. 1980. $3.00.
11. (BOOKSELLER'S CATALOGUE). Oak Knoll Books. *Catalogue 25: Bibliography 26:* [about 2000 items]; *Books About Books* [513 items]. New Castle, Del.: (414 Delaware St, Zip 19720). Summer 1980. Inquire.
12. (BOOKSELLER'S CATALOGUE). Wm. Reese Co. *Catalogue 2: Americana* [406 items]. Illus. New Haven, Ct: [409 Temple St, Zip 06511], 1980. Inquire.
13. *British Library News.* Monthly, from the Press and Public Relations Section, British Library, Stove St. London WC1E 7DG. London. Free
14. *Calligraphy, Medieval: Its History and Technique,* by Marc Drogin, Foreword by Paul Freeman. Numerous Illus. xvii, 198pp. Montclair N.J.: Allanheld & Schram [36 Park St., Zip 07042], 1980. $25.00.
15. *Canada, Historical Atlas of.* Announced. For information, address Audrey M. Livernois, University of Toronto Press, Toronto, Ont. Canada M5S 1A6.
16. *Censorship in America, A Decade of:* the Threat to Classrooms and LIbrarians, 1966–1975, by L. B . Woods. 183pp. Metuchen, N.J.: Scarecrow Press, 1979. $10.00.
17. (CEREMONY, ROYAL). Lant, Jeffery L. *Insubstantial Pageant:* Ceremony and Confusion at Queen Victoria's Court. 270pp. N.Y.: Taplinger Publishing Co., 1980. $12.95.
18. *Children's Books, The Audience for:* a Symposium Sponsored by The Center for the Books and the Children's Literature Center, Held at the Library of Illus. Congress, March 12–13, 1979 (Center for the Book Viewpoint series, No. 2). 42pp. Washington: Library of Congress, 1980. Inquire.
19. (COLOR PLATES.) Bennett, Whitman. *A Practical Guide to American Nineteenth Century Color Plate Books* (1949). xx, 140pp. [New Castle, Del.: Oak Knoll Books (414 Delaware St., Zip 19720), 1980]. $32.50.

20. (COMMUNAL GROUPS). Fogarty, Robert s. *Dictionary of American Communal and Utopian History.* xxvi, 271pp. Westport, Ct: Greenwood Press, 1980. $29.95.

21. (COMMUNICATIONS). Blum, Eleanor. *Basic Books in the Mass Media:* an Annotated Select Booklist . . . 2d Edn. [1179 items]. xi, 427pp. Urbana: University of Illinois Press, 1980. Price?

22. *Crashaw, Richard, A Concordance to the English Poetry of,* Comp. by Robert M. Cooper . . . . lix, 477pp. Troy, N.Y.: Whitston Publishing Co. [P.O. Box 958, Zip 12181], 1981. $35.00.

23. *Dances, Notated Theatrical:* Recorded in Labanotation, Benesh, Movement Notation, Eshkol-Wachman Movement Notation. 21pp. N.Y.: Dance Notation Bureau, Inc. (505 Eighth Ave, Zip 10018), 1980. Inquire.

24. (DARWIN). *The Red Notebook of Charles Darwin.* Ed., With an Introduction and Notes by Sandra Herbert. Illus., incl. Facs. 164pp. Ithaca: Cornell University Press, 1980. $19.50.

25. *Death in Literature,* Ed. by Robert F. Weir. 451pp. N.Y.: Columbia University Press, 1980. $25; $10, paper.

25A. *Dictionary, Oxford American.* Ed. by Eugene Ehrlich et al. xvi, 816 double-columned pp. N.Y.: Oxford University Press, 1980. $14.95.

26. *Directories, The Directory of:* an Annotated Guide to Business and Industrial Directories, Professional and Scientific Rosters, and Other Lists and Guides of All Kinds. First Edition. James M. Ethridge, Editor. 722 double-columned pp. Detroit: Gale Research Co., 1980. $56.00.

27. (EDINBURGH). Royle, Trevor. *Precipitous City:* the Story of Literary Edinburgh. Illus. 210pp. N.Y.: Taplinger Pub. Co, 1980. $14.95.

28. (FAULKNER). *William Faulkner's Gifts of Friendship:* Presentation and Inscribed Copies of Louis Daniel Brodsky, by Louis Daniel Brodsky and Thomas Verich [Catalogue of a Selection Exhibited in the . . . William Library, The University of Mississippi . . .]. Illus. Unpaged. One of 1000 copies. University of Mississippi, 1980.

29. (FURNITURE). McClelland, Nancy. *Duncan Phyfe and the English Regency, 1795-1830.*(1939). Profusely Illus. xxix, 364pp. N.Y.: Dover Publications, 1980. $7.50.

30. *Garcia Marquez, Gabriel:* an Annotated Bibliography, 1974-1979, Comp. by Margaret Eustella Fau. xi, 198pp. Westport, Ct: Greenwood Press, 1980. $27.50.

31A. (HALLUCINOGENS). Hofmann, Albert. *LSD, My Problem Child.* Trans. by Jonathan Ott. xiii, 210pp. N.Y.: MrGraw-Hill, 1980. $9.95.

32. (HALLUCINOGENS). Schultes, Richard Evans, & Albert Hofmann. *Plants of the Gods:* Origins of Hallucinogenic Use. Profusely Illus., incl. color & color plates. 192pp. N.Y.: McGraw-Hill, 1980. $34.95.

33. (HALLUCINOGENS). Wasson, R. Gordon. *The Wonderous Mushroom:* Mycolatry in Mesoamerica. (Ethnomycological Studies, No. 7). Profusely Illus. xxvi, 248pp. N.Y.: McGraw-Hill, 1980. Paper, $12.95.

34. Hansen, Mark. *The Royal Facts of Life:* Biology and Politics in Sixteenth-Century Europe. Illus. 353pp. Metuchen, N.J.: Scarecrow Press, 1980. $16.00.

35. *Herbs and Spices:* the Pursuit of Flavor, Ed. by Waverly Root. Numerous Illus., incl. Color. 191pp. N.Y.: McGraw-Hill Book Co., 1980. $19.95.

36. (HISTORIOGRAPHY). Kammen, Michael, ed. *The Past Before Us:* Contemporary Historical Writing in the United States. Edited for the American Historical Association. 524pp. Ithaca: Cornell University Press, 1980. $19.95.

37. (HISTORIOGRAPHY). Saum, Lewis O. *The Popular Mood of Pre-Civil War America.* (Contributions in American Studies, No. 46) xxiv, 336pp. Westport, Ct: Greenwood Press, 1980. $29.95.

39. *Holmes, Sherlock, The International:* a Companion Volume to The World Bibliography of Sherlock Holmes and Dr. Watson, by Ronald Burt De Waal. [6135 items. 621pp. Hamden, Ct: Archon Books, 1980. $57.50.

40. *Incunabula in the University of Illinois Library at Urbana-Champaign*, Comp. by Marian Harman. (Robert B. Downs Publication Fund, No. 5). 251 double-columned pp. Urbana: University of Illinois Press [1979]. $25.00.

41. (INDIANS). Beidler, Peter G. & Marion F. Egge. *The American Indian in Short Fiction:* an Annotated Bibliography. [880 items.]. xi, 203pp. Metuchen, N.J.: Scarecrow Press, 1979. $10.00.

42. (KU KLUX KLAN). Fisher, William H. *The Invisible Empire:* a Bibliography of the Ku Klux Klan. 202pp. Metuchen, N.J.: Scarecrow Press, 1980. $10.00.

43. *Latin America and the Caribbean*, A Bibliography of: The Hilton Library, by Ronald Hilton. [11,000 items; not annotated or indexed]. 675pp. Metuchen, N.J.: Scarecrow Press, 1980. $29.50.

44. (LIBRARIES). Edelman, Hendrik & Dan C. Hazen. *Collection Development and Management at Cornell:* an Interim Report . . . July 1977-June 1977. [52pp.]. Ithaca: Cornell University Libraries, 1979. Inquire.

45. LIBRARIES). Lane, Alfred H. *Gifts and Exhange Manual.* Illus. with Facsimile Forms. 121pp. Westport, Ct: Greenwood Press, 1980. $15.00

46. (LIBRARIES). *METRO Directory of Members, 1980/81.* 115pp. N.Y.: New York Metropolitan Reference and Research Library Agency (33 West 42 St., Zip 10036), 1980. Inquire.

47. *Libraries, World Guide to* . . . 5th Edn. xxv, 1030 double-columned pp. N.Y.: K.G. Saur [175 Fifth Ave., Zip 10010], 1980. $163.00.

48. *Library Resources, Academic Research and:* Changing Patterns in America, by Charles B. Osburn (New Directions in Librarianship, No. 3). xx. 187pp. Westport, Ct: Greenwood Press, 1979.

49. (LITERARY CRITICISM). Boulton, Marjorie. *The Anatomy of Literary Studies:* an Introduction to the Study of English Literature. 197pp. Boston: Routledge & Kegan Paul, 1980. $20.00.

50. *McCullers, Carson:* a Descriptive Listing and Annotated Bibliography of Criticism, by Adrian M. Shapiro and others. (Garland Reference Library of the Humanities, Vol. 142). Illus. 315pp. N.Y.: Garland Publishing Co., 1980. $35.00.

51. *Madness in Literature,* by Lillian Feder. xvi, 331pp. Princeton: Princeton University Press, 1980. $17.50.

52. *Manuscript Collections:* Initial Procedures and Policies. (*History News,* October 1980, Technical Leaflet 131) Illus. 12pp. Nashville: American Association for State and Local History, 1980. Inquire.

53. (MATERIA MEDICA). Coon, Nelson. *Using Plants for Healing:* an American Herbal (1963). Illus. xii, 272pp. Emmaus, Pa: Rodale Press, 1979. $7.95.

54. (MILITARY FICTION). Smith, Myron J., Jr. *War Story Guide:* an Annotated Bibliography of Military Fiction. [3917 items]. xii, 437pp. Metchen, N.J.: Scarecrow Press, 1980. $20.00.

55. (MOUNTAINEERING). Cox, James R., comp. *Classics in the Literature of Mountaineering and Mountain Travel* from the Francis P. Farquhar Collection of Mountaineering Literature: an Annotated Bibliography . . . [Limited to 500 copies]. 58pp. Los Angeles: University of California Library, 1980. $25.00.

56. (MUSIC). Newcomb, Anthony. *The Madrigal at Ferrara, 1579-1597.* (Princeton Studies in Music, No. 7). 2 vols. Princeton: Princeton University Press. 1980. $60.00.

56A. *Music, Church:* an International Bibliography, by Richard Chaffey von Ende. [5445 items]. xx, 453pp. Metuchen, N.J.: Scarecrow Press, 1980. $22.50.

57. (NATURAL HISTORY.) Brooks, Paul. *Speaking for Nature:* How Literary Naturalists From Henry Thoreau to Rachel Carson Have Shaped America. Illus. with Drawings by the Author. xvi, 395pp. Boston: Houghton Mifflin, 1980. $12.95.

58. (NATURAL HISTORY). Scott, Peter. *Observations of Wildlife.* Prefusely Illus. in Color by the Author. (A Phaidon Book). 112pp. Ithaca: Cornell University Press, 1980. $19.95.

59. *New Orleans, Lost,* by Mary Cable. (Lost [city's name] series). Profusely Illus. 235pp. Boston: Hougton Mifflin, 1980. $21.95.

60. *New York City Notes on Natural History* (serial). Issued five times a year by Sidney Horenstein, Inc. N.Y.: Sidney Horenstein, Inc. (P.O. Box 11, Inwood Station, Zip 10034), V.d. $6.00 a year.

61. *Oral History Evaluating Guidelines:* Report of the Wingspread Conference, July 27–28, 1979, Racine, Wisconsin. 14pp. Denton, Texas: Oral History Association (P.O. Box 13734, NTSU Station, Zip 76203), 1980. Inquire.

62. *Oral History Review, The,* 1980. Port. 129pp. Denton, Texas: Oral History Association (P.O Box 13734, NTSU Station, Zip 76203), 1980. Inquire.

63. (PALEOBOTANY). Andrews, Henry N. *The Fossil Hunters:* In Search of Ancient Plants. Illus. 421pp. Ithaca: Cornell University Press, 1980. $28.50.

64. Pennyroyal, MCMLXXX. [Catalogue Celebrating sixteen titles published in ten years]. Handsome woodcuts on title-page and last leaf. Edition limited to 1000 copies. [Northampton, Mass.: Barry Moser, 1980]. Distributed.

65. (PHILATELY). Kyle, R.A. & M.A. Shampo, eds. *Medicine and Stamps.* Profusely Illus. 2 vols. Huntington, N.Y.: Robert E. Krieger Publishing Co., 1980. $20.00.

66. (PSYCHIATRY). Simon, Bennett, M.D. *Mind and Madness:* the Classical Roots of Modern Psychiatry. (1978). Illus. 336pp. Ithaca: Cornell University Press, 1980. $6.95.

67. *Railway Prints, Early:* British Railways From 1825 to 1850, by Gareth Rees. (A Phaidon Book). Numerous Color and Other Plates. 128pp. Ithaca: Cornell University Press, 1980. $35.00.

68. *Rubens, Peter Paul, The Oil Sketches of:* a Critical Catalogue. Vol. I, Text (698pp. and 71 Plates); II, 24 Color Plates, 504 Plates in Black and White; no text. (National Gallery of Art, Kress Foundation Studies in the History of European Art, No. 7). Princeton: Princeton University Press, 1980. $125.00.

69. *Sea. The, Books On.* Chapter & Verse Catalogue 31. [580 items]. Illus. 101pp. Bristol, R.I.: The Current Co. [P.O. Box 46, Zip 02809]. 1980. $7.50.

70. *Steinbeck, John:* a Collection of books & Manuscripts Formed by Harry Valentine of Pacific Grove, California. [Catalogue Eight, 700 items; Bradford Morrow]. Illus. 154pp. Santa Barbara, Calif.: Bradford Morrow [P.O. Box 4725], 1980. Inquire.

71. (TRANSLATIONS). [Bookseller's Catalogue]. Literature [a series, with "Translations of American and British Authors"]. Illus. Pagination varies. Austin, Texas: Walter Reuben Co. [Suite 910, American Bank Tower, Zip 78701], 1979/80. Inquire.

72. *Utopias:* the American Experience. Ed. by Gairdner B. Moment & Otto F. Kraushaar. Illus. 251pp. Metuchen, N.J.: Scarecrow Press, 1980. $12.50.

73. *Van Bechten, Carl . . . :* a Centenary exhibition of Some of His Gifts to Yale, [an exhibit] Arranged by Donald Gallup. (*Yale University Library Gazette,* Vol. 55, No. 2, Oct 1980). Illus. [48pp.]. New Haven: The Library, 1980. $3.50.

74. *Whitman, Walt, Among the French:* Poet and Myth, by Betsy Erkkila. 296pp. Princeton: Princeton University Press, 1980. $16.50.

75. *Writer's & Photographer's Guide to Newspaper Markets,* by Joan & Ronald Long, xx, 130pp. Costa Mesa, Calif.: Helm Publishing Co. (P.O. Box 10512, Zip 92627), 1980. $9.95.

BOOKS OF INTEREST TO SPECIAL COLLECTIONS OF ALL KINDS PART TWO*

Guides to Collections and Resources

Certainly the two largest books to be noticed this quarter are the component "Author/Title" and "Subject" volumes of the *Guide to Microforms In Print* (81A). We note the 1980 edition, but cite the 1981 edition (and prices) to be published while this issue of *Special Collections* is printing. The *Guide* is a cumulative annual listing of microform titles of all kinds—books, journals, newspapers, government publications, archival material, *collections,* and other projects currently available from micropublishing organizations throughout the world, with the exception of theses and dissertations. The "Subject" volume lists the same titles alphabetically by author under 135 appropriate classification groupings. Addresses are listed in each volume, providing another extremely useful reference source; prices are given, and types of microforms are keyed to them. ALA's *Science Fiction Story Index* (101), in its second edition, 1950–1979, includes citations to many anthologized reprints of stories published before 1950; even Plato, Voltaire, Hawthorne, and Poe are "referenced." This volume will be discussed more fully in the Winter issue of *Special Collections,* which will be devoted to S/F. The "Cumulative Index" volume (15) to Gale's various *Contemporary Authors* sets and related volumes is a tremendous boon for owners of any of these series, all of which have become essential reference tools for different kinds of collections. The "Cumulative Index" includes over 65,000 entries. The 16th annual edition, 1981, of *National Trade and Professional Associations of the United States and Canada* (42), lists the usual helpful information of many difficult-to-locate organizations not gathered in other sources. The book includes about 6,500 organizations, but only those with *national* membership, and excludes

---

*See note at head of preceding section.

fraternal, sporting, patriotic, hobby, and political action groups. Many listings show the 1981 and 1982 places and dates of annual meetings. There is a well-organized index of groupings by reasonable subjects, a geographic index, and an index in ten budget categories from under $10,000 to over $5,000,000, which can be a helpful approach to possible sources for appeals to support special collections. Now in its 4th edition, the *Directory of American Book Specialists* (24) provides another of those many and more and more complete listings of antiquarian dealers and their addresses by area or specialization. This particular *Directory* is an ever-growing useful one with several hundred subjects, but, as with all of their genre, missing some of the most obvious—probably many who did not want to reply or be listed. None of these guides is wholly duplicative of another (while few list private collectors), and someone will eventually try an even more "complete" record, which would include libraries. One of the troubles with all these dealer directories is, of course, the maddening lack of cross-references and the inconsistencies between subject entries; for example, here, two wholly different lists for "Medicine & Medical Books - Modern, Early, Rare" and "Medicine - History". A short-title catalogue to the *Morris H. Saffron Collection of Books on Historical Medicine* (79) is an attractive and nice appreciation of the collecting efforts of a generous practitioner and collector of discriminating professional taste. Only a few of the 528 entries are annotated, but there are some illustrations from the books and a chronological index from 1517 to 1797, as well as a subject index. Among indexes of an historicobiobibliographical nature (as one might call it) is the published form of Yale Professor Benjamin Nangle's tremendous card file of *The "Gentleman's Magazine" Biographical and Obituary Notices, 1781–1819* (56), which continues Farrar and Wheatley's indexes (1886 and 1891) covering the first fifty years of the *GM*, 1731 to 1780. There are approximately 17,000 single-line name entries, coded to the *GM* and its Parts, giving name, occupation or other designation, date of death, and page reference to the original notice. An encyclopedic work and a good place to find 18th to 19th century reference clues, mostly concerning British persons who won't be in the *DNB*.

Dictionaries, Encyclopedias, Atlases, and Other Reference Books, Including Histories of Particular Subjects

There can be no question that the most important book noticed in this review article is Etta Arntzen and Robert Rainwater's *Guide to the Literature of Art History* (13), issued by the ALA in February, though imprinted 1980. This long-awaited updating of Mary Chamberlin's *Guide* (1959) includes and revises about forty percent of Chamberlin's entries but describes several thousand additional works for serious students of art history, while still excluding monographs on individual artists but sometimes including important exhibition catalogues. Organization is based on Chamberlin's, with modifications, and most titles are in Western languages, or with English translations whenever possible; the cut-off date is 1977, with a few important later titles included. Even the smallest library that partakes of interlibrary loan services and has any interest in art (and most art forms) can use this tremendous reference book to great advantage. This book really must be in any such library. It has been worth waiting for, however impatient we may have become, and it will be very satisfying for many years. A guide to another art form is found in *The Literature of Jazz* (60), the 2d edition of a heavily annotated ALA book essential to any modern music collection. Chapters include surveys and bibliographies of literature about the Blues; histories of jazz; lives of jazz musicians; theory and criticism; reference sources; jazz education; jazz in novels, poetry, plays, and films; and jazz periodicals both current and dead. There are good name and title indexes. Policy and practise in the field, though with a distinctly but not exclusively British slant, is described in Joan Clegg's *Dictionary of Social Services* (105), where one can find good summaries of many terms that may conflict with American usage or confuse American readers. There is an exceptionally complete four-page list of "Abbreviations in Common Use in the Social Services." The multilingual, multivolumed *Dictionary of Beekeeping Terms* (19) issued by the International Bee Research Association is an astonishing compilation of columnar vocabularies (not really dictionaries since there are no definitions). It would seem that volumes 1–4 (1951–71) may be out of print or are superseded by 5, 6, and 7, which cover the same languages, with additional 8, English-French-Italian-Spanish-Portuguese-Romanian, and 9, English-Russian-Bulgarian-Serbian-Czech-Polish, in preparation. This great project, and the bee bibliography noted further on, are only partial reflections of the interesting worldwide research into the history and science of beekeeping of which so many of us are wholly unaware. The shame is that here again our language deficiencies keep us ignorant of important work going on elsewhere.

A very practical glossary comes from the Library of Congress's Hebraic Section, *Diplomatic Hebrew* (59B), by Lawrence Marwick. Thousands of Hebrew-English entries are aligned, without definitions, according to the Hebrew word (there is no English-Hebrew section), followed by a 75-page list of Acronyms (mostly Hebrew-Hebrew), and a list of International Associatons, Organizations, and Treaties (Hebrew-English). One of the major publications in the literature of historical bibliography or bibliographical history of the past quarter-century is Roe & Frederick's *Dictionary of Theoretical Concepts in Biology* (20A), citing the theories, laws, and rules of biological concepts, the relative field of the science is noted (not necessarily with definitions), followed by the original and most important references to appear in the literature, either monographic or serial. *A Collector's Dictionary* (35) is a thin work with a miscellany of terms, many of which are disputable and most of which can be found in other sources; it has some incomplete but interesting lists (couches; Chinese terms; gem cuts; stones, i.e., gemstones; etc.), illustrations (such as those of coronets; hallmarks), but is really not a very good book by an apparently retired diplomat. Also peculiar, is Goodier's *Dictionary of Painting and Decorating* (12), unusual in that it "covers also allied industrial finishes." However, there are no chemical formulae to make definitions explicit. Solutions to technical trade problems are sometimes suggested. This book is essentially for British users, but introduces terms creeping into American and Canadian technical vocabularies, and thereby it is probably a worthy purchase for related technical collections.

It is fun to try to find a character, place, or incident not described in *Who's Who in Sherlock Holmes* (102), which is not only a pleasing reference work but pretty nearly complete. Some of the sites or people in the titles of a few stories are not included: one can find Wisteria Lodge but not the Empty House, from the "Adventures of . . . . . . ," the same names; there may be a few others, but this is carping. It is an excellent book.

The World Today Series (all listed under 120) is an unusually up-to-date, annually revised, collection of large-size reference books dealing with different continents or geographic areas of the world. Separate countries are noted with their individual geographical and statistical data, cultural analyses and rather extended histories (nearly to date), with emphasis on political change. Illustrated with clear outline maps, portraits, and excellently selected photographs, each paperbound volume is written by a well-known authority. I have often wondered whether such an inexpensive series might not be a successful publishing project, and now here it is. I hope it can really hang in there and find adequate support through its subscribers because it will serve many purposes in special collections and other library and teaching departments.

Archaeology has many fascinating aspects, but probably none is so attractive to the layperson as *Digging Up Bones* (10A), described in a semitechnical handbook for the physical anthropologist, and even for the amateur digger who might find human remains in his backyard barrow. This authoritative British Museum guide tells about excavating and reporting on human bones, their description and study, measurement and analysis, how to recognize injuries and disease (palaeopathology), and a long bibliography. Somewhat more modern African anthropology is described in Francis Deng's *Dinka Cosmology* (1) representing a fine report of opinions and traditions commented upon by outstanding chiefs and elders of all major divisions of the Dinkas of the Sudan. This expression of the conflicts between tradition and modernity, and their interrelationship with recent history, is extremely interesting for the ethnologist, political scientist, and economist. Two other books describe *Soviet Asian Ethnic Frontiers* (97), and *Central Asians Under Russian Rule* (96). The first ranges from the central steppes to the borders of the Orient and describes "how major states interact with ethnic minorities living along their frontiers," economically, socially, and culturally. It also treats of how this interaction has affected their continued viability as national groups reflecting the political role that frontierland ethnicity plays in the modern world. The book contains, as its last chapter, "A Conversation with Owen Lattimore," full of humanity and sympathetic understanding. Elizabeth Bacon's volume, the second one, is a reprinting of the anthropologist author's residence and exciting travel in the Soviet Union and Kazakstan in 1933–1934, an ethnological classic, originally published in 1966 including the results of her subsequent researches outside the USSR. The new 1980 paperback edition has an updated bibliography throughout the extensive footnotes to Michael Fischer's new Introduction.

Last year saw the publication of the first volume of an encyclopaedic four-volume Official History of the Royal Canadian Air Force. The first volume, Professor S.F. Wise's *Canadian Airmen and the First World War* (16), is a brilliant review of the excellence and heroism of Canadian flyers, organization of the corps, and the birth of airpower everywhere. This scholarly study is a new approach to special considerations of the strategies of WWI and early realizations of the importance of tactically applied air power in different theatres of war though aviation was still in its infancy. There is a lot about individual airmen, "aces," the effect of their idiosyncrasies, Canadian and British politics, etc. The folding military maps and many photographs are unusual. This will really be a monumental set for military, political, and aviation collections.

Changes in the American scene through the centuries are reflected in a group of highly specialized studies of considerable interest to special collections. Some are scholarly, and others are addressed to popular appeal. A few of these are included under other heads in this report, and a few are gathered together here. First is *The Mapping of America* (76), published with the usual excellence of Harry N. Abram's colorplate books, although some illustrations do not come out well and others seem curiously selected. Two of the country's leading map experts, Seymour I. Schwartz, a collector, and Ralph E. Ehrenberg, of the Library of Congress, have joined here to comment on the historical development of the continent, illustrated by 223 maps, 84 in full color, and other illustrations. This is a new overall insight to discovery and exploration, with a most readable text and inspiring maps to tell the story, while not a terribly useful book. Second is Lyle Koehler's comprehensive study of women's status in Puritan New England, *A Search for Power* (118), containing his distinctive analysis of male domination, the inhibition of the female persona, and "the need to keep women down." This is an exciting and revelatory book that is not sensational but is very unusual reading about sexism, sexuality, marital relations, and religious controversy, with much on witchcraft in Salem and elsewhere. Radicalism showed its face too in *The Modern School Movement* (17), which is a history of some aspects of both anarchism and education in the United States in those highly experimental years after the execution of the unconventional educator Francisco Ferrer in Spain in 1909, the rise of the Ferrer Association, the experiments of the Modern School rebels in New York and Shelton, and the impact of the libertarian movements in later years, even into the Seventies and today. Collectors of typography and the book arts will enjoy the chapter initial illustrations originally done by Rockwell Kent for *The Modern School Magazine*. Radicals appeared in the American religious community also, and the excitement, impress, doctrinal change, and political import of the Holiness Movement and its deep-rooted fanaticism is captured in Melvin Dieter's *The Holiness Revival of the Nineteenth Century* (46A), which like Koehler's *A Search for Power* (above; 118) makes dramatic reading for anyone interested in the intellectual and social history of our nation. Similarly, twenty-four papers by qualified scholars describe *America and Ireland, 1776–1976* (6) in their compound study of the American identity and the Irish connection, as a bicentennial event celebrating the strength of the Irish-American consciousness. Contributions of the Irish to every aspect of American life are reviewed—from politics, religion, labor, and the military, to literature, music, and the theatre. These are easy, undocumented readings full of the glory of the subject and most informative. A somewhat comparable lot of essays by specialist authorities is *The Arts in Canada* (28), surveying the past fifty years, though the book limits itself mostly to literature, poetry, art, music, and the theatre.

Many other books that are listed following these notices deserve careful perusal by special collections and reference librarians. I cannot close this section, though, without comment on a few other books that describe the passing American scene—one, the mill, as described in *Mills of Wisconsin and the Midwest* (82), is a lovely book with on-site pencil or charcoal drawings and colorplate paintings, and a text describing the early mills, mills in motion, the building of the old mills, millstones and rollers, saw mills and others, a list of mills to visit, etc. Another book, compiled from photographs selected from the collections of the Library of Congress, *A Century of Photographs, 1846–1946* (89A), while not exclusively pictures of America, gives an intimation of the tremendous resources available through the Library, and the interesting stories and events that might be revealed through research in any collection of visuals. Then, just for fun, I will remind readers of the reprint edition of *Clean and Decent* (121), a history of the bath and loo, in Great Britain, France, and America, with some delightful illustrations but no graffiti. The changing American and British society of cultured persons' manners and taste in the last three hundred years has never been made so real for me as in the fully illustrated book, *Fads and Fancies* (47), an intelligent selection by Denys Sutton of his edited overtures to various issues of the art periodical *Apollo*. The frivolous and the moral are brought into balance here, while progress or change in artistic display, cultural habits, and the patron-artist relationship, are all commented upon with humor and understanding.

Bibliographies and Specialist Booksellers' Catalogues

Essays describe and bibliographies list the foreign influences of earlier writers on American fiction through Henry James in David Kirby's *America's Hive of Honey* (49). Like a detective story the references press into the past to analyze hidden origins of themes, characters, placements, and sometimes the stories themselves. An intricate mosaic torn apart, with derivations traced and analyzed. Scholars of English and Continental Romanticism will wallow with satisfaction among the hundreds of fully annotated writings in *The Romantic Movement* (94),

MLA's committees' selective and critical bibliography for 1979, which attempts to include, with descriptive and critical annotations, all books and articles "of substantial interest to scholars"; English, French, German, and Spanish literatures are covered.

The mention of detective stories leads, quite naturally, to *Crime Fiction Criticism* (38), an annotated bibliography that supplements and supersedes much of what has been done before. It contains more than 2000 entries covering numerous subjects and the writings of over 250 individual authors. Curiously, there are more entries on Dickens than any other author, though Dickens is not generally thought of in this genre. There's lots of Sherlock Holmes, too, of course, and nearly everyone else is represented. The citations are complete and the annotations excellent. Unannotated but subjectively complementary is *Crime, Detective, Espionage, Mystery, and Thriller Fiction & Film* (37), a comprehensive bibliography of critical writing through 1979. Some material, especially that concerning films, and the other than English language pieces, do not appear in the previously noted book. The author arrangement, with title and subject indexes is helpful, but most libraries will opt for *Crime Fiction Criticism* (38) and its annotations, which is easier to use and has meaningful annotations.

Few of us, I believe, have had any idea of the quantity of works produced by Paul Rosenfeld, but Charles Silet's extensive annotated bibliography, *The Writings of Paul Rosenfeld* (95), includes over four hundred books, translations, collections, articles, and reviews from 1907 to 1970, including reprints, of course. Hundreds of letters are listed and over 200 "Writings about [him]." Amost every item of the four hundred by him is described and reflects the wide range of his creativity, learning, and careful thought. *Walt Whitman and the Critics* (115) is not as usefully constructed and is only an extensive but unannotated checklist of criticism about him from 1900 to 1978, by hundreds of authors cited in 2752 entries. There is a name index of coauthors, editors, and translators, and an extensive subject index.

It is so easy to get lost in thought reading the annotations in *British Bee Books: a Bibliography, 1500–1976* (18), especially the references to earlier books and earlier bees! This attractive and illustrated book of over 800 titles is highly instructive, very careful in its bibliographical techniques, its description of 32 'Metaphorical Titles, 1662 to 1974," short-title index, and subject index. Further, it locates each volume listed, including three American libraries' holdings—Cornell, Wisconsin, and LC. There is an unusual index providing a chronological list of children's books and beekeeping. Even more lively action than reading the annotations to bee books is to learn about Scarecrow Press's ambitious new plan for a series on "Native American Bibliography," of which *Bibliography of the Sioux* (59C) is the first number issued, leading the score or more scheduled on the American Indian for the 1980s. A sensible arrangement of the 3367 entries in the first volume under specialized chapter headings, the limitations (and extensions) of inclusiveness, and the complete name index, suggest how useful the entire series will be for students and libraries if the same format is retained.

Not to be ignored as a major contribution to Latin American bibliography is the large volume *Reference Materials on Latin America in English: The Humanities* (62A), by Richard D. Woods, with its 1252 entries, nearly all with very extensive annotations, fully indexed by author, title, and a refined, detailed subject analysis. It is unusual—but ideal—to have such elaborate annotations. Would that all publishers might encourage them. Fortunately, all entries are numbered, and the author's authority can be cited bibliographically as "Woods 283" when quoting his detailed appraisals of books. Similar comments can be made about *Changes in American Society* (56A), where entries refer exclusively to official government publications—federal, state, municipal—a kind of reference work too often neglected by even the most serious writers. The selection of documents here almost exclusively concern the social problems of people. The annotations, once more, are compact statements of contents.

Two Canadian book selection tools that have come my way deserve mention, especially as our nations' interests complement one another and find greater need for mutual understanding. *Canadian Selection: Books and Periodicals for Libraries* (21), in its 1977–1979 supplement, is an annotated guide to significant English language books and periodicals for adults, published in Canada, about Canada, or written by Canadians at home or abroad. Choice has been for small and medium-sized public libraries, but colleges and schools will benefit from consideration. Nearly 2000 titles are listed. Classified by Dewey Decimal System, full bibliographical information and costs are given, as are suggested library subject headings. *Canadian Books for Young People* (30) is a similar volume but without subject headings and with a different classification of separate subjects.

Booksellers' catalogues—at least the ones we received—were not outstanding recently for this column's purposes, except for The Jenkins Company's catalogue of *The Whole World* (24), and *The South, the Civil*

War, Negroes, and Slavery (106), the former being a most attractively designed quarto-size volume with over a thousand unusual items of fairly priced but also fairly expensive pieces—perhaps nothing under $200, and from that on up; the second catalogue of 200 items, also fully annotated, runs from $20 pieces to some of several thousand dollars, though most are in the lower price range. So much history in the notes to both. We are all used to the attractively printed catalogues of John Howell-Books, and *Americana Catalogue 52* (8) is no different; however, it is the shop's first one wholly devoted to the subject (excluding the famous California ones). Most inviting features are the many unusual maps from the collection of George Davidson, renowned California surveyor, mostly with his notes. Lots of classics here—Audubon, *Walden,* and such—but the catalogue encompasses a lot of extraordinary books seldom met with. Upcroft Books, Winchester, England's Catalogue 25 (112) is Part One, A–K, with M–Z coming later, altogether over a thousand books on "The Tudors and the Stuarts," with many out-of-the-way items priced inexpensively. This is quite a departure from Upcroft's regular series on the Middle Ages.

Two specialist dealers' catalogues serve as important bibliographical reference tools: first, *The Two Russian Revolutions* (98A) from Dekker & Nordemann, Amsterdam, a catalogue for the sale of the collections of Leon Bernstein and Boris Souvarine. Considerable value attends the catalogue for its corrections of numerous bibliographical details lacking, incomplete, or in error in other lists that include some of these publications. Secondly, a very unusual, brief, but interesting and varied offering of some extremely scarce and not inexpensive items offered for sale appear in the "Short-Title List of Botany/Pharmacology" (26) of Biblion, Inc., for which detailed descriptions will be sent on request. This is a sensible and relatively inexpensive way to issue a catalogue for persons who might be seriously interested in particular pieces.

Special Collections and Archival Administration

Tremendously important is Richard J. Wolfe's *Early American Music Engraving and Printing* (117A): a History of Music Publishing in America From 1787 to 1825, With Commentary on Earlier and Later Practices, which is published in cooperation with the Bibliographical Society of America, a landmark book by a scholar-librarian-bibliographer. The work is innovative, thorough, revealing, and important to the history of music, musicology, engraving, and publishing studies of the United

States. Brilliantly conceived and written with style, much information is uncovered and coordinated for the first time. The book is essential for any collections of printing, publishing, music, and Americana.

We have received a new edition, with an updated bibliography, of Ullman's *Ancient Writing and Its Influence* (77), necessary for study by anyone dealing with early manuscripts. Particularly helpful are the latter chapters on abbreviations and ligatures, numerals, and writing materials and practices. A practical book of specialized interest is *Alexander the Great and the Greeks* (5), by A.J. Heisserer, a detailed application—a study manual for the epigrapher, if you will—concerning all of the stele and fragmentary evidence and their proper dating referring to Alexander and the Greeks. Methodology, translations, and other evidence, all well illustrated, make good historic reading and even better practical examples for the student epigrapher.

Law collections will want to keep the 23 February 1981 issue of *AB Bookman's Weekly* (63) for Timothy E. Knier's "The Secondhand Market in Law Books: a Dealer Survey" in which, for the first time, we have a sound analysis of the book stock specialties and services of the law book antiquarian trade, with a summary of what makes it tick, buying and selling, how to select dealers, and how to nurture them to the best advantage.

Percy G. Adams has written a new introduction to his 1962 book, *Travelers and Travel Liars, 1660-1800* (111), a companion bibliography-reader for all literature and travel collections that relate to the period. It is a thrilling story of travel, imagined travel (not imaginary voyages), and ratiocination, too good to be missed by any bookperson. Another delightful item demonstrates that Edgar Rice Burroughs' Tarzan series is really "literature" in the best tradition. And it is proved by a Professor of Classics at that! What a pleasure it is to find that *Tarzan and Tradition* (110) justifies our reading, as the subtitle says, of the "classical myth in popular literature" even beyond our simple enjoyment. Analyses of the language, technique, animals, hero, and themes all justify the conclusion that ERB knew exactly what he was doing and did it well in the Homeric mode.

A hero for special collections librarians (though not as exciting as Tarzan, of course) is described in the biography and writings of *Justin Winsor, Scholar-Librarian* (65), who was nine-times President of the ALA, and whose work and personality, developed at the Boston Public Library and Harvard, gave lustre to librarianship as a profession. A more modern and frank book about a recently retired hero to many of us is

Ellsworth On Ellsworth (65A). Seldom modest and always forthright, the practical aspects of Ellsworthianism are set forth here for all of us to revel in, and we can learn from his accomplishments and admitted mistakes. Here is a great man of our own times and a fine librarian whose contributions will have lasting effects.

BOOKS RECEIVED

All books received are listed here. Titles marked with an asterisk (*) have been commented upon in the preceding bibliographical essay. Listing does not preclude further notice in subsequent issues. Prices are listed when known.

*1. (Africa). Deng, Francis Mading. *Dinka Cosmology.* 348pp. London: Ithaca Press, 1980. $12.50.

2. *Albert the Great:* Commemorative Essays. Ed., With an Introd. by Francis J. Kovach & Robert W. Shahan. Port. xix, 297 pp. Norman: University of Oklahoma Press, 1980. $12.95.

3. *Albinus on Anatomy,* by Robert Beverly Hale & Terence Coyle. 208pp. Profusely Illus., with Albinus' Plates and Diagrammatic Analyses. N.Y.: Watson-Guptill Publications, 1979. $19.95.

4. (Alchemy). Nicholl, Charles. *The Chemical Theatre.* Facs. Illus. 292pp. Boston: Routledge & Kegan, Paul, 1980. $35.

*5. *Alexander the Great and the Greeks:* the Epigraphic Evidence, by A.J. Heisserer. Illus. xxvii, 252pp. Norman: University of Oklahoma Press, 1980. $29.95.

*6. *America and Ireland, 1776–1976:* the American Identity and the Irish Connection. The Proceedings of the United State Bicentennial Conference of Cumann Merriman, Ennis, August 1976. Ed. by David Noel Doyle & Owen Dudley Edwards. xvii, 348pp. Westport, Ct: Greenwood Press, 1980. $25.

7. (American Village). *The Short Season of Sharon Springs:* Portrait of Another New York. Original Photographis by Hansi Durlach. Text by Stuart M. Blumin & Deborah Adelman Blumin. Photographs. 128pp. Ithaca: Cornell University Press, 1980.

*8. *Americana:* John Howell, Books. Catalogue 52—A Selection of Printed and Manuscript Materials Relating to the Western Hemisphere, Hawaii, and the Philippine Islands. Illus. 282pp. San Francisco: John Howell (434 Post Street, Zip 94102), 1980. $ Inquire.

9. (Anthropology). Gallaher, Art. Jr., & Harland Padfield (School of American Research Advanced Seminar Series). xiv, 305pp. Albuquerque: University of New Mexico Press, 1980. $25.

*10. (Anthropology). Nutini, Hugo G. & Betty Bell. *Ritual Kinship:* the Structure and Historical Development of the Compadrazgo System in Rural Tlaxcala. Vol. I. Map & Diagrs. xvi, 494pp. Princeton: Princeton University Press, 1980. $28.50; 11.50.

*10A. (Anthropology, Physical). Brothwell, Don R. *Digging Up Bones:* the Excavation, Treatment, and Study of Human Skeletal Remains. 2d Edn. (British Museum, Natural History, 3rd Edition, Publication No. 704). Illus. 196pp. London: British Museum, Natural History: [distr: Rudolph Sabbot, P.O. Box 772, Woodland Hills, Calif., 913648, 1972. $7.

11. (Art). Bouleau, Charle. *The Painter's Secret Geometry:* a Study of Composition in Art. Pref. by Jacques Villon [Trans. From the French by Jonathan Griffin]. (1963). Profusely Illus. 268pp. N.Y.: Hacker Art Books, 1980. $30.

*12. (Art). Goodier, J.H. *Dictionary of Painting and Decorating:* Covers Also Allied Industrial Finishes . . . [2d Edn]. 308pp. High Wycombe, Bucks. (Crendon Street), 1974. US$.

*13. *Art History, Guide to Literature of,* by Etta Arntzen & Robert Rainwater. 616pp. double-columns. Chicago: American Library Association, 1980. $75.

*13A. *Artifacts and the American Past*, by Thomas J. Schlereth. Illus. 204pp. Nashville: American Association for State and Local History (1400 Eighth Ave, Zip 37203), 1980. $13.95; AASL Members, $10.50.

14. (Auction Catalogue). *Wertvolle Bucher, Manuskripte, und Autographen, Alte und Moderns Kunst, Dekorative Graphik Gemalde*. 101 Auktion, 11–13 Dezember 1980. [6079 lots]. Illus. 578pp. Hamburg: F. Dorling, 1980. DM20.

*15. *Authors, Contemporary:* Cumulative Index, Includes References to All Entries in *CA*. Vols. 1–88; *CA* Permanent Series, Vols. 1–2, and *Contemporary Literary Criticism*, Vols. 1–11; *Something About the Author*, Vols. 1–16; *Authors in the News*, Vols. 1–2. 167 four-columned pp. [over 65,000 entries]. Detroit: Gale Research Co., 1980. Free to subscribers?

*16. (Aviation). Wise, S.F. *Canadian Airmen and the First World War:* the Official History of the Royal Canadian Air Force, Vol. I. (Published in Cooperation With the Department of National Defense and the Canadian Government Publishing Centre, Supply and Services Canada). Illus., incl. Fold. Maps, etc., Some Colored. xx, 771pp. Toronto: University of Toronto Press, 1980. $35.

*17. Avrich, Paul. *The Modern School Movement:* Anarchism and Education in the United States. Illus., incl. Ports. xiii, 447pp. Princeton: Princeton University Press, 1980. $30; 12.50.

*18. *Bee Books, British:* a Bibliography, 1500–1976, by [the] International Bee Research Association: Joan P. Harding, et al. Illus. 270pp. Gerrards Cross, Bucks. (Hill House, SL9, ONR): The Association, 1979. US$30.

*19. *Beekeeping Terms, Dictionary of.* International Bee Research Association; With Allied Scientific Terms. Ed. by Eva Crane. Vol. 5: English-French-German-Russian-Spanish, With Latin Index (206pp.; $11.50); 6: English-Finnish-Hungarian, With Latin Index (104pp.; $6.90); 7: English-German-Dutch-Danish-Norwegian-Swedish, With Latin Index (238pp.; $13.80). Gerrards Cross, Bucks: The Association (Hill House, SL9 ONR), 1977; 1978; 1978. $As above.

20. (Biblical Typology). Landow, George P. *Victorian Types, Victorian Shadows:* Biblical Typology in Victorian Literature, Art, and Thought. xiii, 266pp. Boston: Routledge & Kegan Paul, 1980. $24.95.

*20A. *Biology, Dictionary of Theoretical Concepts in,* by Keith E. Roe & Richard G. Frederick. xli, 267pp. Metuchen, N.J.: Scarecrow Press, 1981. $17.50.

*21. (Book Selection). McLean, Isabel, comp. *Canadian Selection:* Books and Periodicals for Libraries, 1977–1979 Supplement. [6155 plus items]. 398pp., double-columns. Toronto: University of Toronto Press, 1980. $27.50.

*22. *Book Specialists, Directory of American:* [Sources for Antiquarian and Out-of-Print Titles. 4th Edn.], R.H. Patterson, Editor. 190pp. N.Y.: Continental Publishing Co. (1261 Broadway, Zip 10001), 1981. $Inquire.

23. *Books, Continental Printed, 1480–1700.* Catalogue 160 [251 items]. Illus. 85pp., double-columns. London: E.P. Goldschmidt (64 Drayton Gardens, SW10 9SB), 1980. Request.

*24. (Books & Manuscripts). *The Whole World:* Books and Manuscripts on Many Subjects. Catalogue 128 [1174 items]. By John Jenkins, et al. Illus. Unpaged. Austin: The Jenkins Co., 1980. Inquire.

25. *Boston, Lost,* by Jane Holtz Kay. Illus. by Over 300 Photographs and Prints. 304pp. Boston: Houghton Mifflin, 1980. $24.95.

*26. Botany/Pharmacology, Short Title List [96 items; not annotated]. 4pp., stapled. Forest Hills, N.Y.: Biblion, Inc., Booksellers (P.O. Box 9 Zip 11375), 1980. Request.

27. (Canada). Radford, Tom, ed. *Alberta, a Celebration.* Stories by Rudy Wiebe; Photographs in Color by Harry Savage. 208pp. Edmonton, Alberta: Hurtig Publishers (10560 - 105th St), 1979. $29.95. Canadian.

*28. *Canada, The Arts in:* the Last Fifty Years, Ed. by W.J. Keith & B.-Z. Shek. Illus. 157pp. Toronto: University of Toronto Press, 1980. $20; 6.95.

29. *Canada, The Mountains of,* by Randy Morse. Introd. by Andy Russell. Profusely

Illus. in Color. 144pp. Edmonton, Alberta: Hurtig Publishes (10560 105th St), 1979. $29.95 Canadian.

*30. *Canadian Books for Young People*, Ed. by Irma McDonough. 205pp. Toronto: University of Toronto Press, 1980. $15.

31. Carson, Rachel. *The Sea Around Us*. Introd. by Maitland A. Edey. Illus. With Colored Frontis. and Photographs by Alfred Eisenstaedt. xxix, 252pp. N.Y.: Limited Editions Club [551 Fifth Ave., Zip 10017], 1980. Membership. Inquire.

32. *Cat Poems, Some of the*, by Artie Gold. Illus. 28pp. [Woodhaven, N.Y.8 Cross Country Press (P.O. Box 21081, Zip 11421), 1978. $2.

33. *Chaucer's "Troilus and Criseyde" and the Critics*, by Alice R. Kaminsky. Frontis. 245pp. Athens: Ohio University Press, 1980. $15.

33A. *Children's Faces Looking Up:* Program Building for the Storyteller, by Dorothy de Witt. 156pp., double-columns. Chicago: American Library Association, 1979. $11.

34. *Christmas Carols, The International Book of*. (1963). Musical Arrangements by Walter Ehret; Translations and Notes by George K. Evans. Illus. 338pp. Brattleboro, Vt: The Stephen Greene Press, 1980. $12.95.

35. *Collector's Dictionary, A*, by Henry Hainworth. Illus. 119pp. Boston: Routledge & Kegan Paul, 1981. $14.95.

36. *Cookbook, Wofford College*. 59pp. Spartanburg, S.C.: [The Sandor Teszler Library, Wofford College, Zip 29301]. $Inquire.

*37. *Crime, Detective, Espionage, Mystery, and Thriller Fiction & Film:* a Comprehensive Bibliography of Critical Writings Through 1979. Comp. by David Skene Melvin & Ann Skene Melvin. 367pp. Westport, Ct: Greenwood Press, 1980. $29.95.

*38. *Crime Fiction Criticism:* an Annotated Bibliography, Ed. by Timothy W. Johnson & Julia Johnson et al. (Garland Reference Library of the Humanities, Vol. 233). xii, 423pp. N.Y.: Garland Publishing. 1981. $40.

39. *Dee, John:* the World of an Elizabethan Magus, by Peter J. French (1972; reissue). Port. & Other Illus. 243pp. Boston: Routledge & Kegan Paul, 1980. $25.

40. *Delacroix, Eugene, The Journal Of*. Trans. From the French by Walter Pach. (1937). 731pp. N.Y.: Hacker Art Books, 1980. $50.

41. (Detective Literature). *Cross Country*, No. 10/11: a Poetic Investigation of Detectives, Mystery, and Murder. Ed. by Robert Galvin et al. 88pp. Woodhaven, N.Y.: Cross Country Press (P.O. Box 21081, Zip 11421), 1978. Trimonthly; two-year subscription $12.

*42. (Directory). *National Trade and Professional Associations of the United States and Canada, and Labor Unions*, 16th Annual Edition. Ed. by Craig Colgate, Jr. 416pp., triple-columns. Washington, D.C.: Columbia Books, Inc. (777 14th St, N.W., Zip 20005), 1981. $35.

43. *Elizabethan Grotesque*, by Neil Rhodes. 207pp. Boston: Routledge & Kegan Paul, 1980. $30.

44. *Encyclopaedia of the Middle Ages, Renaissance, and Reformation*. Ed. by Nicholas Mann et al. [Announced for 1981 - . 20 vols.] Leiden: E.J. Brill, 1981 - . $Inquire.

45. (England). Whittle, Tyler. *Victoria and Albert at Home*. Illus. xix, 212pp. [Boston:] Routledge & Kegan Paul, 1980. $19.50.

46. *English Dissent:* Catalogue To an Exhibition of Eighteenth Century Pamphlets, 18 October to 18 November 1979 . . . , by Margaret A. Howell & Charles F. Mullett. Facs. & Other Illus. 116pp. Columbia, Mo.: Ellis Library, University of Missouri/Columbia, 1979.

*46A. (Evangelicalism). Dieter, Melvin Easterday. *The Holiness Revival of the Nineteenth Century*. (Studies in Evangelicalism, No. 1). 356pp. Metuchen, N.J.: Scarecrow Press, 1980. $17.50.

*47. *Fads and Fancies*, by Denys Sutton. Introd. by Kenneth Clark. Profusely Illus. 240pp., double-columns. N.Y.: Wittemborn & Co., 1979. $25.

48. *Fausey, Jessie Redmon, Black American Writer,* by Carolyn Wedin Sylvander. Ports. 275pp. Troy, N.Y.: Whitston Publishing Co., 1981. $18.50.

*49. (Fiction, American). Kirby, David. *America's Hive of Honey;* or, Foreign Influences on American Fiction Through Henry James: Essays & Bibliographies. xvii, 214pp. Metuchen, N.J.: Scarecrow Press, 1980. $12.50.

50. *Filing Rules, ALA,* by the Filing Committee, Resources and Technical Services Division, American Library Associaton. 50pp. Chicago: American Library Assocation, 1980. Paper, $3.50.

51. *First Editions:* Catalogue 5. [490 items]. 40pp. London: Minerva Rare Books (252 Brockley Road, SE4 2SF), 1981. Request.

52. Flaubert, Gustave, *The Temptation of Saint Anthony.* Trans., With an Introd. and Notes by Kitty Mrosovsky. Illus. 293pp. Ithaca: Cornell University Press, 1980. $19.50.

53. (Food & Drink). Edmunds, Lowell. *The Silver Bullet:* the Martini in American Civilization. (Contributions in American Studies, No. 52). Illus. xviii, 149pp. Westport, Ct: Greenwood Press, 1981. $19.95.

54. Garcia Lorca, Federico. *The Cricket Sings:* Poems and Songs for Children. Trans. by Will Kirkland. Illus. by Maria Horvath. Unpaged. N.Y.: New Directions, 1980. $4.95.

55. *Gauguin, Paul, Sculpture and Ceramics of,* by Christopher Gray. (1963). Numerous Illus., incl. Color Plates. 330pp., double-columns, N.Y.: Hacker Art Books, 1980. $75.

*56. *The Gentleman's Magazine:* Biographical and Obituary Notices, 1781–1819— an Index, by Benjamin Nangle. Introd. by Stephen Parks. (Garland Reference Library, Vol. 212). 422pp. N.Y.: Garland Publishing, 1980. $55.

57. *The Harvard Crimson Anthology:* 100 Years at Harvard. Ed. by Greg Lawless, '75. Illus. xix, 378pp. Boston: Houghton Mifflin, 1980. $16.95.

58. *Hassam, Childe,* by Donelson F. Hoopes. 32 Color Plates & Other Illus. 88pp., double-columns. N.Y.: Watson-Guptill Publications, 1979. $20.

59. *Hassam, Childe, 94 Prints by.* Selected & Introduced by Joseph S. Czetochowski. 90pp. N.Y.: Dover Publications, 1980. $6.

59A. Hazlitt, William. *Liber Amoris; or, the New Pygmalion:* an Authentic Story of the Two Faces of Love. Ed., With an Introd. and Notes by Gerald Lahey. (Gotham Library Series). Port. & Facs. 266pp. N.Y.: New York University Press, 1980. $17.50; 8.

*59B. *Hebrew, Diplomatic:* a Glossary of Current Terminology. Comp. by Lawrence Marwick. 188pp. Washington, Library of Congress [distr: Supt. of Documents, GPO], 1980. $8.50.

*59C. (Indians). Marken, Jack W. & Herbert T. Hoover. *Bibliography of the Sioux.* (Native American Bibliography Series, No. 1). xvi, 370p. Metuchen, N.J.: Scarecrow Press, 1980. $17.50.

*60. *Jazz, The Literature of:* a Critical Guide, by Donald Keenington & Danny L. Read. 236pp. Chicago: American Library Association, 1980. $11.

61. (Jones, Le Roi). Laey, Henry C. *To Raise, Destroy, and Create:* the Poetry, Drama, and Fiction of Imamu Amiri Baraka (Le Roi Jones). xii, 205pp. Troy, N.Y.: The Whitston Publishing Co., 1981. $15.

62. *Keats, Metamorphosis in,* by Barry Gradman. xx, 140p. N..: New York Universty Press, 1980. $14; 6.

*62A. *Latin America, Reference Materials on,* in English: the Humanities, by Richard D. Woods. xii, 639pp. Metuchen, N.J.: Scarecrow Press, 1980. $32.50.

63. "Law Books, The Secondhand Market in Law Books: a Dealer Survey," by Timothy E. Knier. *(AB Bookman's Weekly,* Vol. 67, No. 8, 23 Feb. 1981, pp. 1371–89). Clifton, N.J.: Antiquarian Bookman (P.O. Box AB, Zip 07015), 1981. Single issue, $3.

64. Lehnus, Donald J. *Book Numbers:* History Principles, and Application. Tables, etc. 153pp. Chicago: American Library Associaton, 1980. Paper, $7.50.

*65. (Librarian). Cutler, Wayne & Michael H. Harris. *Justin Winsor, Scholar-Librarian.* (The Heritage of Librarianship Series, No. 5). 196pp. Littleton, Colo: Libraries Unlimited, 1980.

*65A. (Librarian). Ellsworth, Ralph E. *Ellsworth on Ellsworth:* . . . "Library Science" and Me, Since Our Confluence in 1931 . . . . Illus. 163pp. Metuchen, N.J.: Scarecrow Press, 1980. $9.50.

66. (Librarianship). Cheney, Frances Neel & Wiley J. Williams. *Fundamental Reference Sources.* 2d Edn. 351pp. Chicago: American Library Association, 1980. $12.50.

67. (Librarianship). Fleischer, Eugene & Helen Goodman. *Cataloguing Audiovisual Materials:* a Manual Based On the Anglo-American Cataloguing Rules II. Illus. 388pp. N.Y.: Neal-Schuman, Publishers, 1980.

68. (Libraries). Dolnick, Sandy, ed. *Friends of Libraries Sourcebook.* Illus. x, 165pp. Chicago: American Library Association, 1980. $6.

68A. (Libraries). Jackson, Eugene B., ed. *Special Librarianship:* a New Reader. 759pp. Metuchen, N.J.: Scarecrow Press, 1980. $27.50.

69. (Libraries). Rochella, Carlton C., ed. *An Information Agenda for the 1980s:* Proceedings of a Colloquium,. June 17–18, 1980. 119pp. Chicago: American Library Associaton, 1981. $6.50.

70. (Libraries). Spoor, Richard D. *The Shape of Things to Come:* Union Theological Seminary Library, New York City—a Planning Document. 2d Edn, Rev. Illus. With Diagrs. and Tables. 76 leaves. N.Y.: Union Theological Seminary [Library] (99 Claremont Ave, Zip 10027), 1978. Inquire.

71. *Libraries, Free Magazines for,* by Adeline Mercer Smith. xxi, 258pp. Jefferson, N.C.: McFarland & Co. (Box 611, Zip 28640), 1980. $16.95.

72. *Library Administration, Local Public.* Completely Rev. by Ellen Altman, ed., in Cooperation With the International City Management Association. 2d Edn. 251pp., double-columns. Chicago: American Library Association, 1980. $20.

73. *Library Display Ideas,* by Linda Campbell Franklin. Illus. xiv, 230pp. Jefferson, N.C.: McFarland & Co. (Box 611, Zip 28640), 1980. $11.95; 7.95.

74. (Library of Congress). Hilker, Helen-Anne. *Ten First Street, Southeast:* Congress Builds a Library, 1886–1897. An Exhibition . . . of the . . . Library of Congress. Numerous Illus. 102pp., double-columns. Washington: Library of Congress (distr: Supt. of Documents, GPO, Zip 20402), 1980. $4.75.

*74A. *McCullers, Carson:* a Descriptive Listing and Annotated Bibliography of Criticism, by Adrian M. Shapiro et al. (Garland Reference Library of the Humanities, Vol. 142). 315pp. N.Y.: Garland Publishing Co., 1980. $35.

75. *Manuscripts, Early, & Illuminated Leaves.* Catalogue Twelve [62 items]. Illus. 60pp. Southport, Ct: (181 Old Post Road, P.O. Box 490, Zip 06490), 1980. Request.

*76. *The Mapping of America,* by Seymour I. Schwartz & Ralph E. Ehrenberg. Illus., incl. Color; Maps, etc. 363pp., double-columns. N.Y.: Harry N. Abrams, 1980. $60.

*77. (MART): Christopher Dawson. *Mission to Asia.* (Medieval Academy Reprints for Teaching, 8). xli, 246pp. $6; John Gower. *Confessio Amantis.* Ed. by Russell A. Peck. (MART, 9) xlvii, 525pp. $7.95; B.L. Ullman. *Ancient Writing and Its Influence.* Introd. by Julian Brown. (MART, 10). Illus. xviii, 224pp. $7.50. Toronto: University of Toronto Press, 1980. $Various.

78. (Medical History). Winslow, Charles-Edward Amory. *The Conquest of Epidemic Disease:* a Chapter in the History of Ideas (1943). 411pp. Madison: Univesity of Wisconsin Press, 1980. $25; 7.50.

*79. *Medicine, Historical, Morris H. Saffron Collection of Books on:* a Short Title Catalogue. Presented by the Academy of Medicine of New Jersey to the George F. Smith Library of the Health Sciences, College of Medicine and Dentistry of New Jersey. [Helene Goldstein, Cataloguer]. Illus. 70pp., double-columns. Newark: Smith Libary, CMDNJ (100 Bergen St., Zip 07103), 1980. Request.

80. *Meredith, George:* a Reappraisal of the Novels, by Mohammad Shaheen. 150pp. Totowa, N.J.: Barnes & Noble Books, 1981. $19.50.

81. *Michelangelo and the Language of Art,* by David Summers. 68 Illus. xvii, 626pp. Princeton: Princeton University Press, 1981. $42.50; 16.50.

*81A. (Microforms). Voegelin-Carleton, Ardis, ed. Guide to Microforms In Print. [Vol. I:] Author/Title; [II:] Subject. Incorporating International Microforms In Print. 2 vols. Westport, Ct: Microform Review, Inc., 1981. Author/Title, $84.50; Subject, $89.50.

*82. *Mills of Wisconsin and the Midwest,* by Jerry Apps & Allen Strang. Illus. With Original Drawings and Color Plates of Paintings [by Allen Strang]. 128pp., double-columns. Madison, Wisc.: Tamarack Press (P.O. Box 5650, Zip 53705), 1980. $12.50.

83. *Minnesota's Boundary With Canada, Its Evolution Since 1783,* by William E. Lass. (Minnesota Historical Society. Public Affairs Center Publications). Illus., incl. Ports. & Maps in Color. 141pp., double-columns. St. Paul: Minnesota Historical Society, 1980. $16.50; 8.75.

83A. (Moving Pictures). Goldstein, Ruth M. & Edith Zornow. *The Screen Image of Youth*: Movies About Children and Adolescents. Illus. xix, 363pp. Metuchen, N.J.: Scarecrow Press, 1980. $20.

84. Muir, John. *To Yosemite and Beyond:* Writings From the Years 1863 to 1875. Ed. by Robert Engberg & Donald Wesling. Illus., incl. Ports. & Facs. 171pp. Madison: Univesity of Wisconsin Press, 1980. $17.50: 5.95.

85. (Music). Camner, James, ed. *The Great Instrumentalists in Historic Photographs:* 274 Portraits From 1850 to 1950. 148pp. N.Y.: Dover Publications, 1980. $6.95.

86. *New Mexico Magazine's Enchanted Trails,* by Ruth Armstrong and the Staff of the . . . Magazine. Illus., incl. Maps & Trails. 249pp. Sante Fe: New Mexico Magazine, 1980. $7.95.

87. (New York State). *Bedford Tricentennial, 1680-1980.* Articles On the History of Bedford in Westchester County . . . From Its Beginnings As a Settlement of the Colony of Connecticut, by Donald W. Marshall, Town Historian. Illus. 69pp. Bedford Hills N.Y.: [Town House, Zip 10507], 1980. $3.75.

88. O'Neill, Eugene. *Poems, 1912-1944.* Ed. by Donald Gallup. 119pp. New Haven: Ticknor & Fields, 1980. $9.95.

89. Perrin, Noel. *Second Person Rural:* More Essays of a Sometime Farmer. Illus. 152pp. Boston: David R. Godine, 1980. $10.

*89A. *Photographs, A Century of,* 1846-1946: Selected From the Collections of the Library of Congress. Comp. by Renata V. Shaw. Profusely Illus. 211pp. Washington: Library of Congress [distr: Supt. of Documents, GPO], $9.

89B. *Photography Books Index:* a Subject Guide to Photo Anthologies, by Martha Moss. Frontis. 286pp. Metuchen, N.J.: Scarecrow Press, 1980. $15.

90. (Poetry). Brown, Merle E. *Double Lyric:* Divisiveness and Communal Creativity in Recent English Poetry. 236pp. N.Y. Columbia University Press, 1980. $20.

91. *Poets, Fifty American, A Reader's Guide to,* by Peter Jones. (Reader's Guide Series). 386pp. Totowa, N.J.: Barnes & Noble, 1980. $16.50.

92. (Policy Planning). Barker, Anthony, comp. *Public Participation in Britain:* a Classified [and Annotated] Bibliography. [1387 items]. Published In Association With The Royal Town Planning Institute. xvi, 192pp. London: Bedford Square Press, National Council of Social Service [distr: Renouf/USA, Old Post Road, Brookfield, Vt, Zip 05036], 1979. $17.40.

93. (Private Press Books). Irving, Washington. *The Legend of Sleepy Hollow,* With Nineteenth-Century Illustrations. 46pp. Branford, Ct: The Penny-Whistle Press, [distr: The Antiquarium, 66 Humiston Drive, Bethany, Ct 06525], 1980. $30, pre-paid.

*94. *Romantic Movement, The:* a Selective and Critical Bibliography for 1979. Ed. by David V. Erdman et al. xxvii, 333pp. N.Y.: Garland Publishing Co., 1980. $35.

*95. *Rosenfeld, Paul, The Writings of:* an Annotated Bibliography, by Charles L.P. Silet. Foreword by Lewis Mumford. Port. & Facs. xxx, 214pp. N.Y.: Garland Publishing Co., 1981. $35.

*96. (Russia). Bacon, Elizabeth E. *Central Asians Under Russian Rule:* a Study in Cultural Change. Introd. by Michael M.J. Fischer. Illus., incl. Maps. xxxix, 273pp. Ithaca: Cornell University Press, 1980. Paperback only. $5.95.

*97. (Russia). McCagg, William O., Jr. & Brian D. Silver, eds. *Soviet Asian* Ethnic Frontiers. (Pergamon Policy Studies On the Soviet Union and Eastern Europe Series). Maps xx, 280pp. N.Y.: Pergamon Press, 1979. $32.50.

98. *Russian Literature:* an Inroduction, Robert Lord. 213pp. N.Y.: Taplinger Publishing Co., 1980. $9.95.

98A. *Russian Revolutions, The Two:* Catalogue . . . An Exceptional Collection of Old and Rare Journals, Books, and Pamphlets, Mainly From the Libraries of Leon Bernstein and Boris Souvarine. [1188 items]. Ports. and Other Illus., incl. Facs., and 2 Color Plates. 188pp. Amsterdam: Dekker & Nordemann (distr: Philadelphia: D & N Library Services, 48 East Chestnut Hill Ave, Phila., Pa, 19118), 1980. Inquire.

99. (Science). Reichenbach, Hans. *From Copernicus To Einstein.* Trans. by Ralph B. Win (1942). 123pp. N.Y.: Dover Publications, 1980. $2.

100. (Science Bibliography). Neu, John ed. "One Hundred Fifth Critical Bibliography of the History of Science and Its Cultural Influences, to January 1980." [3585 citations]. (*ISIS*, Vol. 71, No. 260, Critical Bibliography 1980). 295pp. Philadelphia: Dept. of History and Sociology of Science, Univesity of Pennsylvania, 1980.

*101. *Science Fiction Story Index:* Second Edition, 1950–1979, by Marilyn P. Fletcher. 610pp. Chicago: American Library Association, 1981. $20.

*102. *Sherlock Holmes, Who's Who in,* by Scott R. Bullard & Michael Leo Collins. 251pp. N.Y.: Taplinger Publishing Co., 1980. $14.95; 7.95.

103. *Skinner, Constance Lindsay, Author and Editor:* Sketches of Her Life and Character With a Checklist of Her Writings And the "Rivers of America" Series. General Editor Ann Heidbreder Eastman. Ports. & Facs. 83pp. N.Y.: Women's National Book Association [distr: Patterson Smith Corp., 23 Prospect Terrace, Montclair, N.J., 07042], 1980. $9.95.

104. (Social Services). Longley, A.R., et al. *Charity Trustees' Guide.* 32pp. London: Bedford Square Press, National Council of Social Service [distr: Brookfield, Vt: Renouf/USA, Inc. (Old Post Road, Zip 05036)], 1979. $3.15.

105. *Social Services, Dictionary of:* Policy and Practice, by Joan Clegg. [3d Edn]. 148pp. London: Bedford Square Press, National Council for Voluntary Organizations [distr: Brookfield, Vt: Renouf/USA, Inc. (Old Post Road, Zip 05036)], 1980. $12.50.

*106. Spiller, Robert E. *Late Harvest:* Essays and Addresses in American Literature and Culture. (Contributions in American Studies, No. 49). 280pp. Westport, Ct: Greenwood Press, 1981. $25.

107. Spiller, Robert E. *Late Harvest:* Essays and Addresses in American Literature and Culture. (Contributions in American Studies, No. 49). 280pp. Westport, Ct: Greenwood Press, 1981. $25.

108. *Stevenson, Robert Louis:* a Critical Celebration, Ed. by Jenni Calder. Illus. 104pp. Totowa, N.J.: Barnes & Noble Books, 1980. $15.

109. (The Sun). Cole, John N. *Sun Reflections:* Images For the New Solar Age. Numerous Illus. 246pp. Emmaus, Pa: Rodale Press, 1981. $14.95; 10.95.

*110. *Tarzan and Tradition:* Classical Myth in Popular Literature, by Erling B. Holtsmark. (Contributions to the Study of Popular Culture, No. 1). 196pp. Westport, Ct: Greenwood Press, 1981. $22.50.

*111. *Travellers and Travel Liars, 1660–1800,* by Percy G. Adams. (1962). With a New preface by the Author. Illus. xiv, 214pp. N.Y.: Dover Publicatons, 1980. $4.50.

*112. *Tudors and Stuarts, The:* Catalogue 25. Part One—A to K [549 items]. 42pp. Winchester, Hants: Upcroft Books (66 St Cross Rd., SO23 9PS), 1981. Request.

112A. (U.S. Navy). Bryson, Thomas A. *Tars, Turks, and Tankers:* the Role of the United States Navy in the Middle East, 1800–1979. Illus. 269pp. Metuchen, N.J.: Scarecrow Press, 1980. $14.

*113. Wasson, R. Gordon. *The Wondrous Mushroom:* Mycolatry in Mesoamerica. (Ethnomycological Studies, No. 7). 139 Illus., 52 in truly wondrous color; Maps, etc. xxvi, 248pp., 1 leaf. N.Y.: McGraw-Hill, [1980]. Limited to 401 copies for sale. Signed by the author. $525.

114. *Whitman, Walt, and the Critics:* a Checklist of Criticism, 1900–1978, by Jeanetta Boswell. (The Scarecrow Author Bibliographies, No. 51). xiii, 257pp. Metuchen, N.J.: Scarecrow Press, 1980. $14.50.

*115. *Whitman, Walt, and the Critics:* a Checklist of Criticism, 1900–1978, by Jeanetta Boswell. (The Scarecrow Author Bibliographies, No. 51). xiii, 257pp. Metuchen, N.J.: Scarecrow Press, 1980. $14.50.

116. *Wilson, Woodrow, The Papers of.* Vol. 33: April 17—July 21, 1915; Vols. 34, July 21, 1915—Sept 30, 1915. Ed. by Arthur S. Link et al. Illus. 2 vols. Princeton: Princeton University Press, 1980. each, $30.

117. (Wilson, Woodrow). Tribble, Edwin, ed. *A President in Love:* the Courtship of Woodrow Wilson and Edith Bolling Galt. Illus. With Photographs. xxiv, 225pp. Boston: Houghton Mifflin, 1981. $11.95.

*117A. Wolfe, Richard J. *Early American Music Engraving and Printing:* a History of Music Publishing In America from 1787 to 1825, With Commentary on earlier and Later Practices. (Music in American Life Series.) Published in Cooperation With the Bibliographical Society of America. Illus. xix, 321pp. Illinois: University of Illinois Press, 1980. $24.95.

*118. (Women). Koehler, Lyle. *A Search for Power:* the "Weaker Sex" in Seventeenth-Century New England. Illus. With Charts. 561pp. Urbana: University of Illinois Press, 1980. $25.

*119. (Women). Rigney, Barbara Hill. *Madness and Sexual Politics in the Feminist Novel:* Studies in Bronte, Woolf, Lessing, and Atwood. 148pp. Madison: Univesity of Wisconsin Press, 1978. $15; 5.95.

*120. The World Today Series: *Africa, 1980,* by Pierre Etienne Dostert, 140pp; Harold C. Hinton, *The Far East and Southwest Pacific, 1980,* 99pp; John D. Cozean, *Latin America, 1980,* 107pp; Ray L. Cleveland, *The Middle East and South Asia, 1980,* 102pp. Profusely Illus., incl. Ports, Maps, Diagrs. Washington, D.C.: Stryker-Post Publications (888—17th St., N.W., Zip 20006), 1980. Revised Annually. Each. $3.25.

*121. Wright, Lawrence. *Clean and Decent:* the History of the Bath and Loo, and of Sundry Habits, Fashions, & Accessories of the Toilet, Especially in Great Britain, France, & America. [New Edition, With Material by Dave Larder]. Numerous Illus. 211pp. Boston: Routledge & Kegan Paul, 1980. $7.95.

For Product Safety Concerns and Information please contact our EU
representative GPSR@taylorandfrancis.com
Taylor & Francis Verlag GmbH, Kaufingerstraße 24, 80331 München, Germany

www.ingramcontent.com/pod-product-compliance
Lightning Source LLC
Chambersburg PA
CBHW070621300426
44113CB00010B/1617